05/00

05/00

# THE PERIOD SHIP HANDBOOK III

*Keith Julier*

# NEXUS
SPECIAL INTERESTS

Nexus Special Interests Ltd.
Nexus House
Azalea Drive
Swanley
Kent BR8 8HU


First published 2000

ISBN 1-85486-200-6

Photosetting by Stirling Graphics Ltd., Southend

Printed and bound in Great Britain by Whitstable Litho, Kent

# CONTENTS

List of colour plates                                                                     6

Introduction                                                                              7

Chapter 1        The 74-gun *Ship Bellona*                                                 9

Chapter 2        *H.M.S. Unicorn*                                                         33

Chapter 3        The English Brig *Portsmouth*                                            55

Chapter 4        The See Ewer *Elbe*                                                      67

Chapter 5        The Spanish 17th Century 104-gun Ship *San Felipe*                       85

Chapter 6        *H.M.S. Bounty's* Jolly Boat                                            111

Chapter 7        *H.M.S. Victory* - Main Section                                         119

Chapter 8        *The Pride of Baltimore ll 1988*                                        129

Chapter 9        The Armed Transport *Bounty*                                            141

Chapter 10       The American Whaling Brig *Viola*                                        155

Chapter 11       Another Look at Rigging                                                 181

Index                                                                                    189

# LIST OF COLOUR PLATES

(on pages 107 - 110)

HMS *Bellona*

HMS *Unicorn*

The English Brig *Portsmouth*

The 17th Century Spanish 104-gun *San Felipe*

Sea Ewer *Elbe*

*HMS Bounty*'s Jolly Boat

*HMS Victory*

*The Pride of Baltimore 1988*

Armed Transport *Bounty*

The American Whaling Brig *Viola*

# INTRODUCTION

While the basis of this third volume is again the building of period ship models from kits, on this occasion I also introduce the reader to scratch building. The Viola was chosen as a suitable transitional subject, being full of interest and offering a few different challenges to set the model maker thinking, without recourse to any more tools and equipment than those necessary for kit building. This particular chapter is not so much a detailed building instruction, as a guide through the thought processes required to research and plan ahead, so that nothing gets missed or gets presented incorrectly. For instance, what was the design of the American flag in 1910? Can I put boat covers on the whaleboats so that I don't have to present all the boats' internal detail? Get it wrong and you are likely to find that there are a number of people who do know, all of whom will be most pleased to let you know, after the event of course.

I have commented in previous writings about the research, or lack of it, that has been done by some kit manufacturers for their product. I have also read nit-picking comments from some modellers who are of the opinion that, for the money they pay, every tiniest detail should be provided ready made, and to the correct design and size. If you build Viola or, indeed, any simple scratch built model for the first time, I believe that you will better appreciate just what goes into the production of a kit, particularly if your research and acquisition of materials is carried out under any sort of financial restraint. One must always remember, that whatever your needs are as a model maker, the kit is a commercial enterprise to the manufacturer and, at times, a rather delicate balancing act between what the customer ideally wants and what he is prepared to pay.

Having said all that, and considering that I probably make as many kits as anybody, I honestly believe that the kit manufacturers do listen to the feed back from model makers. Certainly, overall, I think that the standard of kits has considerably improved over the years and, in today's fairly cut throat market place, a poor kit just won't sell, and that is of no use to manufacturer nor the model maker. There are not too many kits today where you have to get out the fret saw and certainly the quality of fittings and castings has generally improved no end. As I have said so many times before, no kit is perfect and, as a commercial product, they are never likely to be. But it is no good moaning, however constructively, to your mates at the club. Go public, write to the distributor, write to Model Boats magazine or, if you speak the language concerned, write to the manufacturer. OK, your particular kit may not necessarily be made better by complaining, but ultimately, the voice gets heard and standards will rise. Champions of kit builders everywhere, Euro Models have been one of the louder voices in persuading kit manufacturers to improve their standards and I have, over the years, seen and benefitted from the results of their efforts.

In this volume I have included another chapter with further hints and tips that may help to make life a little easier for the model maker who has some apprehension about rigging his model. There are also notes indicating some of the pitfalls to avoid and descriptions of what some of the major rigging features actually do. Knowledge of rigging is an ongoing process for me: I almost certainly acquire more information with every model that I build. Knowing what a particular run of rope actually does, helps to make more sense of its passage through the maze of other rigging. In a perverse sort of way, it also helps you decide what you can sensibly omit from your particular scale of model. I am always extremely suspicious of the model maker who tells me that he or she has put everything on their model! An artist friend once commented to me that making a model boat is something like painting a landscape. The art is in knowing what detail to leave out.

The reader might also notice that I don't necessarily use wood for wooden parts or metal for metal work. I will use whatever I have to hand that I can reasonably work with to produce an acceptable result. So, my spares box is full of bits of balsa, scraps of plasticard, cardboard etc., which I feel that I can legitimately use to make or enhance my model. Sacrilege, do I hear someone comment? This is probably the same person who will complain that the capstan in their kit has only eight holes and it should have ten! To him I say, building model ships is all about having a good time and that innovation is part of the craft. But, seriously, I have no real quarrel with the modeller who chooses to try to follow the path of perfection. Maybe he can tell me where I can get some scale grained oak!

In the gathering of information and material to build the models on which this book is based, I am indebted to Andrew Horne at Euro Models, Twickenham, Mike Doane at Home

Made Flags and, for continued encouragement and inspiration, to John Cundell at Model Boats magazine. And, of course, none of this would have been possible without the support of my wife who, no longer able to participate in my model making, uncomplainingly puts up with sawdust on all floors, well, for at least ten minutes!

The colour photography of the Viola, Bellona and Bounty is the work of Gary Sinfield, the remaining colour work was done by Manny Cefai, both of whom have a talent of which I am greatly envious.

# CHAPTER I

# THE 74-GUN SHIP *BELLONA*

HMS BELLONA
1780

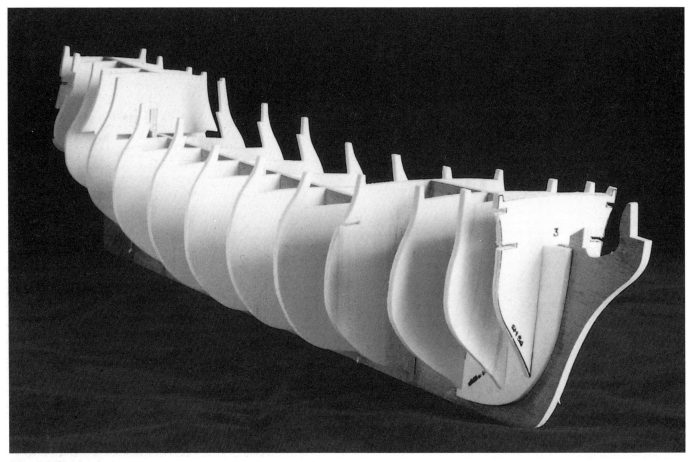

**Fig. 1.1 The basic carcase**

**B**ellona was launched and commissioned in 1760 and a year later was in action against the French 74-gun ship *Courageux* which was captured after a fairly intense battle. From 1764 *Bellona* served as a guard ship at Portsmouth for seven years then was laid up at Chatham before being refitted for Channel service in 1780. This was a major refit and it was at this time that her bottom was first coppered.

During the next twenty years *Bellona* had a chequered career, twice taking part in the relief of Gibraltar under Admirals Howe and Danby, and again serving as guard ship at Portsmouth. After a further refit she served with Howe's fleet in the Channel and had another tour of duty in the West Indies.

Following repairs in 1805, which involved doubling and bracing, she had a further nine years of active service before being broken up at Chatham in 1814.

## The Kit

A well-presented box of materials and drawings with a host of pre-cut parts and fittings. I did find that while the standard of ply used for the hull frames was but adequate, the strip wood and special sectioned timbers were of excellent quality. The drawings were extremely well-draughted and provided a good picture of most phases of construction. A very well-produced sheet of photo-etched parts was also provided, particularly for those ornamental features around the stern galleries. However, there were some shortcomings in the multilingual instruction manual in that some part numbers were incorrectly cross-referenced to the drawings.

The actual design of the kit was very good and, provided that procedures and the parts list sequence were systematically followed, there should be no problems in constructing an excellent model. Oh yes, and Corel do provide you with pre-cut parts for a very practical stand.

The kit describes a model for both before and after the 1780 refit.

The letter "f" was used in the parts list to indicate optional items. Some of these were a bit tricky to make but, rather than leave them off, you may find it better to simplify their application.

The colouring guide requires some careful study, remembering that many parts need to be painted before final assembly. The guide is based on colour priority and has to be scanned very closely to find pertinent part numbers.

## Tools

Nothing too sophisticated was required to build the model, although if the basic kit of craft knife, small saw and light hammer were supplemented by a 12 volt drill and sander, life would be that much easier. For plank bending, a plank nipper was adequate for the majority of the timber although the walnut used for the wales required a more serious heat and soak treatment. The usual various grades of abrasive paper are, of course, essential as are adhesives. There is considerable paint work to be done unless you want to leave everything "as seen" in bare wood and brass. Finally, keeping an oilstone handy to maintain absolute sharpness of your cutting tools will enable a better and safer result to be achieved.

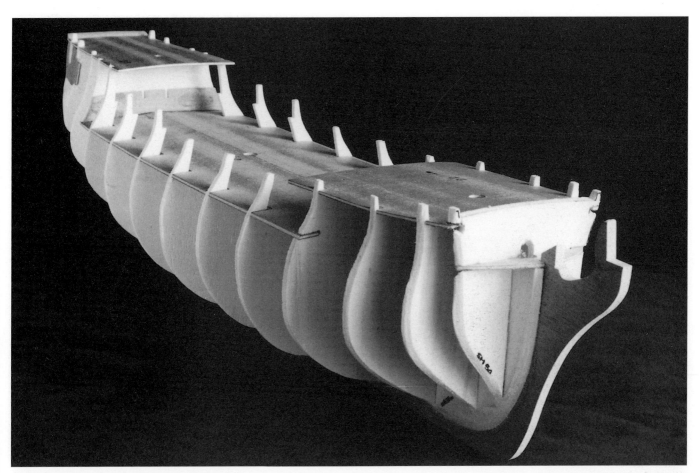

**Fig. 1.2 Three false decks in position.**

**Fig. 1.3 The facing of the forecastle deck.**

Fig. 1.4 Support jig for cutting the "U" section material.

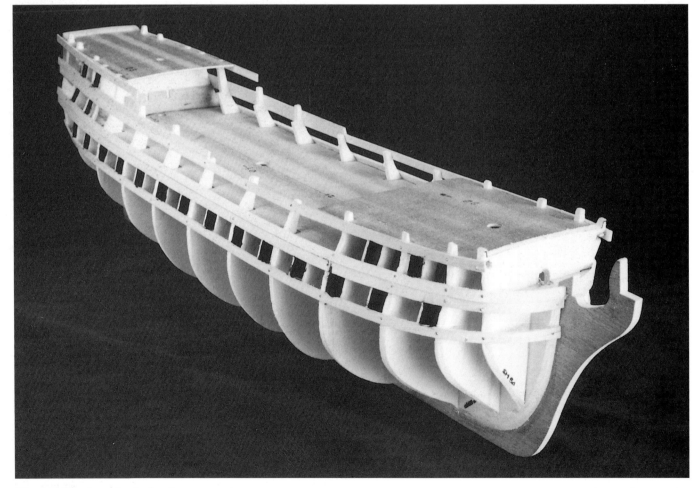

Fig. 1.5 The key planks in place.

**Fig. 1.6 The first planking completed. Note the sweep of planks under the stern.**

**Fig. 1.7 The transom plate in place with support piece for the gallery framework.**

**Fig. 1.8 The framework for the quarter gallery.**

## The Hull Carcase

The conventional kit construction of false keel and slotted frames was followed for this part of the build. Many of the slots were a bit on the sloppy side and, in many cases, needed packing. Having said that, the situation was not disastrous and a strong and stable construction was achieved, see **Fig.1.1**. The deck piece sprang into place over the ears on the top of the frames and it was found that the whole assembly was more manageable if frame 13 was put in place after the deck. The

three decks in place are shown in **Fig.1.2**.

I would stress that it was most important to read the instructions at every stage of the build and, at the same time, check part numbers and descriptions quoted in the parts list. If you don't, you could find yourself putting things in the wrong place or in the wrong order. For instance, the fascia panels for the forecastle and poop decks were very similar in shape and the written instructions were not entirely clear as to what went where. The fascia to the forecastle deck can be seen in **Fig.1.3**

The brackets and supports around the stern section had to be carefully aligned and a dry run was considered essential. When all glue was thoroughly set, the task of shaping the

Fig. 1.9  Basic gallery planking.

Fig. 1.10  The transom facing.

edges of the frames and the filler blocks was carried out. The suggested procedure shown on the drawings was more than adequate, but PermaGrit tools made the job so much easier. One area to which I paid particular attention was the filler block assembly below the stern chaser ports. The planking for the hull undersides sweeps tightly around this area so it was most important to get the curves right to avoid the possibility of breaking a few planks later on.

## The First Hull Planking

Corel have obviously put a lot of thought into the design of the kit, thus, the modeller would be well-advised to take advantage of the sequence of planking specified in the manual. This makes it very easy to ensure that the correct line of the gun-

ports is achieved. Two sizes of "U" sectioned timber were provided to make up the dummy ports on the enclosed gun decks and needed to be cut into short lengths. I would strongly recommend that the lengths of both sizes be cut to 19mm in order to provide more fixing area inside the planking. After unthinkingly trying to saw through the unsupported section, it became apparent that if I wasn't going to split the wood at every attempt, some sort of simple jig was necessary. The scrap box provided a couple of pieces that let me locate the ears of the "U" to stop them flexing under the action of the saw, and a back-up block to absorb the thrust, (**Fig.1.4**). At the same time, I made up a two-plank-width gap gauge by gluing a couple of 35mm lengths of plank material together, edge to edge.

It was essential to get the line of the first plank each side of

Fig. 1.11  Second planking complete down to waterline.

Fig. 1.12 "Copper" plating under way.

Fig. 1.13 Sheathing completed.

Fig. 1.14 Sheathing is applied also to keel and stem. Note also hole for bowsprit.

Fig. 1.15 Main deck fitted out before assembling quarter deck.

**Fig. 1.16 The poop deck with skylight in place.**

the hull in its correct alignment. Once that was pinned and glued in place, the gap gauge guaranteed the run of the remaining planks that delineated the top and bottom edges of the gun-ports, (**Fig.1.5**).

Some of these strips form part of the inner faces of the main deck bulwarks where the ears on frames have to be removed later. These particular strips were carefully pinned to the ears but not glued, again see **Fig.1.5.**

The "U" shaped pieces for the blank ports were then put into place. Some pieces were left as cut, but others had to have one side removed. Don't jump the gun (forgive the pun) look particularly for dotted lines on the drawing to make sure which shape goes where! There are a couple of places where you might anticipate an "L" rather than a "U" shape!

I stuck each of these parts in place initially with cyano-acrylate, the main thing being to get the sides properly vertical. There is not much surface to glue in some cases, hence my choice of adhesive. When I was satisfied that all were in the correct position, I then thoroughly filleted all edges of the pieces at the backs of each assembly with white PVA. It was absolutely essential that maximum strength was attained. Later, holes would have to be drilled to take the dummy gun barrels and it would be fatal at that stage if you pushed a "U" piece off the inside of the hull planking.

Once all glued joints had dried, and tested for soundness, the inside surfaces of the dummy gun-ports were painted matt black. It was easier to do the painting at this stage rather than leave it until later as specified in the instruction manual.

The remainder of the first hull planking was then carried out in the usual way, nothing more than a plank nipper being required to form the necessary bends, even for the more serious bends on those planks that come tight under the stern and finish at a line below the gun-ports for the stern chasers, (**Fig.1.6**). I thought that this was a feature that could have been

shown more clearly on the drawings. However, if you refer to Sheet No.9 - sketches B and E, the line referred to is more apparent. These same sketches also indicate the line which the planking follows below the aftmost frames, ie., where those frames blend in with the false keel.

This latter procedure raised another question. If your model is to represent the vessel prior to the 1780 refit and thus will have its underside planking coated with white stuff, I reckon that you should gradually reduce the thickness of the false keel towards its back edge so that the combined thickness of keel and second planking will be the same as the rudder thickness. The planking can then be trimmed back from the edge of the false keel and vertical strips of second planking put on to simulate the sternpost and everything sanded down in situ.

Alternatively, if the model is to have a coppered bottom, the tapering of the false keel will not be necessary, since the rudder was also coppered and both will finish up the same thickness.

## The Stern Gallery Basic Structure

At the completion of the first planking, the beak deck and front facing were planked. A similar planking procedure for the deck of the stern gallery was carried out, before painting the internal gallery surfaces and etched brass parts. It was important to note that the brass pilasters, whilst identically numbered, were in fact a set of three right hand and three left hand, each of the three being subtly different to match the top and bottom of their associated facings. The transom plate was then fitted and left for the glue to thoroughly set.

The next stage was a mite troublesome, to say the least. The instructions recommended that the quarter gallery framework pieces were assembled without glue, then offered up to establish what cutting and shaping was

Fig. 1.17 The quarter deck with the binnacle in the shelter of the poop deck.

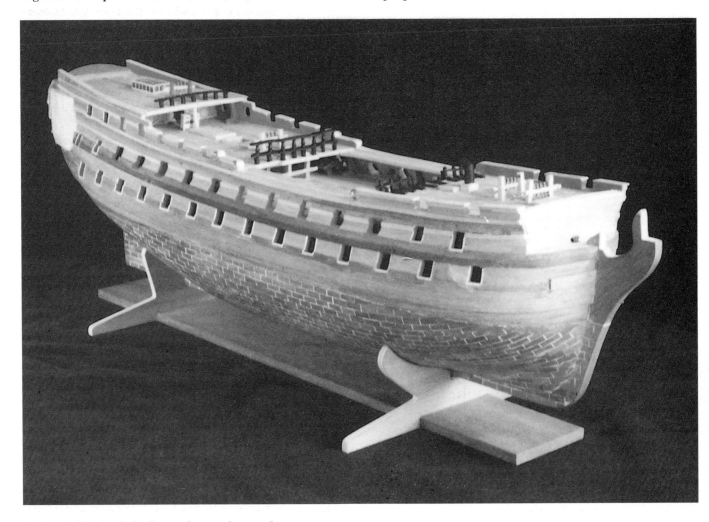

Fig. 1.18 The basic hull complete on its stand.

**Fig. 1.19 The start of the head timber construction.**

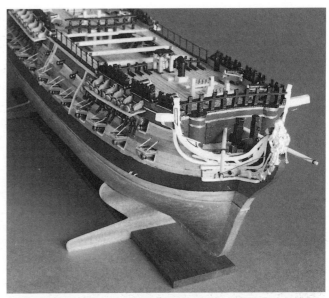

**Fig. 1.20 Headrails complete and figurehead in place.**

required to attain the required fit. Some parts just could not be dry assembled. However, the reasons for the instruction were well-founded, but the end shapes had to be achieved using a different procedure. I shaped the inner pieces relative to the edge of the transom plate and glued them in place, (**Fig.1.7**). The edges of the remaining parts, which sat against the hull side and the inner face of the transom, were then shaped to provide a good fit. It was found that there was considerable excess material to be removed from the curved outer faces of these parts and this was largely removed prior to permanently fixing them in place, (**Fig.1.8**). The final shaping was done in situ after the glue had dried. The planking of the galleries was then carried out as per the instructions, (**Fig.1.9**), followed by the stern surfaces, (**Fig.1.10**).

## The Second Planking

Again, it was important to follow the sequence of planking shown in the instructions as well as to keep an eye on the sizes of timber to be used. The initial key was to get the first "L" shaped moulding in its right place, since the alignment of all of the upper hull planking was dependent upon it. This part of the procedure was straightforward and the thing to watch was that it was best to sand each section of different thickness strip after positioning and before continuing with the next.

Bending the 4 x 2mm strips for the wales could not be satisfactorily accomplished using a plank nipper, the curves round to the stem being too severe. The upper wale comprised two strips per side and I cut each into two pieces, making a scarf joint in the area behind where the anchor bolster would go. The long lengths back to the quarter galleries were put in in one piece, leaving a short length to be bent around the bows. Having made my scarf joint, I then carefully cut across the rear of the short plank using a razor saw, a series of 1mm depth cuts about 3mm apart. The pieces were then boiled in a kettle and left for an hour to soften before attempting to bend, pin and glue them in place. Not the easiest of tasks, but it worked. The main wales, each made up of three 4 x 2mm strips, were made up in the same way.

I did deviate from the advised sequence at this stage, in that

I planked above the first laid "L" shaped moulding, in order to strengthen the first planking in that area. I felt that it would be rather vulnerable to breakage while sheathing the hull below the waterline. The drawings had to be followed carefully when carrying out the upper planking since the instruction manual and parts list were a little bit at odds with each other, mixed up in the selection of 2 x 1mm strip and 2mm "L" shaped moulding. Having proceeded thus far with the second planking, it was time to recognise whether the model was to depict the vessel before or after the major refit of 1780. One of the main differences was the addition of copper sheathing below the waterline. If the "before" option was chosen, then the hull should be planked in the conventional manner from below the main wale down to keel as directed in the instruction manual. If the "after" option was selected, then there were two choices available within the confines of material provided in the kit. You could plank in the conventional way then copper paint the area below the waterline or, if like me you are a glutton for punishment, you could tile the bottom.

First, I marked the waterline position on the surface of the first planking. I then planked conventionally down to, and a little beyond, that line and when the glue had dried, re-scribed the waterline and trimmed the planks to it, (**Fig.1.11**). The copper plates were reckoned to be 48 x 15in so I calculated that at a scale of 1/100 the 4mm wide planking strips in the kit, cut to a length of 12mm, would provide me with a tile within a "gnat's" of being right.

The plates basically followed the same lines as the planks below and would include stealers as necessary in the same manner as planking. To make the plates, a strip of the 4mm wide strip was first chamfered on both edges of one face. The size of the chamfer needed to be only about 0.25mm x 45ʃ some of which would eventually disappear on final rubbing down. However, that was considered enough to provide the required gentle hint of the plate outlines suitable for this scale. The plank was then cut into 12mm lengths. I made a simple cutting jig to get them all identical, but it was found that it would be necessary to occasionally use a slightly shorter or longer plate to compensate for the compound curvature of the hull bottom. Keeping an abrasive sheet to hand on my bench, before I positioned each plate, I introduced chamfers to each of the two short edges. In overall terms, the covering of the

**Fig. 1.21  The forecastle deck with belfry and galley chimney stack.**

**Fig. 1.22  The stern gallery and ornamentation.**

hull bottom took about the same amount of time to cover with the plates as it would have had I planked in the usual way and, of course, didn't use any more material. The start of the plating can be seen in **Fig.1.12**. However, I did finish up with what I thought was a better representation of a coppered hull. Model Lite filler, rubbed in with the fingers, formed a grout between the plates. A light rubbing down prepared the surface for finishing.

The gun-ports were then cut and sized together with the hole for the rudder. The completed plating and cut gun-ports are shown in Figs. **1.13 & 1.14**.

I then made up the stand/cradle to provide a stable support for the hull while working on the next stages of construction. The pre-shaped supports needed no adjustment to match the curves of the hull and very little to provide a good snug fit on the base. A screwed and glued joint was made for each support to ensure a strong enduring cradle.

## The Decks and Fittings

Again, it was essential to follow the sequence of construction laid down in the manual or risk the possibility of suddenly finding yourself in a position where you had blocked off access for fitting something or other.

The upper parts of three of the main frames were removed, the bulwarks lined and the main deck gun-ports opened out. I found that it was worth making up one of the gun carriage assemblies to ensure that the positions of the ports were correct before final sizing. The inside surfaces of the bulwarks were painted red before proceeding to lay the deck.

The deck was planked using 3mm x 0.6mm strip starting from a centrally-aligned king plank. When using such thin material, I find that PVA tends to warp the timber thus making the rubbing down operation a bit of a bind. Cyanoacrylate is a bit too rapid and doesn't give enough time to position things. UHU general purpose adhesive or balsa wood cement overcome both of these shortcomings, although care must be taken to not to use too much and spread it all over the option.

As far as caulking was concerned, I blackened one edge of each planking strip with a chisel-pointed marker pen before assembly. At this scale, marking both edges seemed to be a bit too prominent.

There was quite a bit of work to do before fitting the quar-

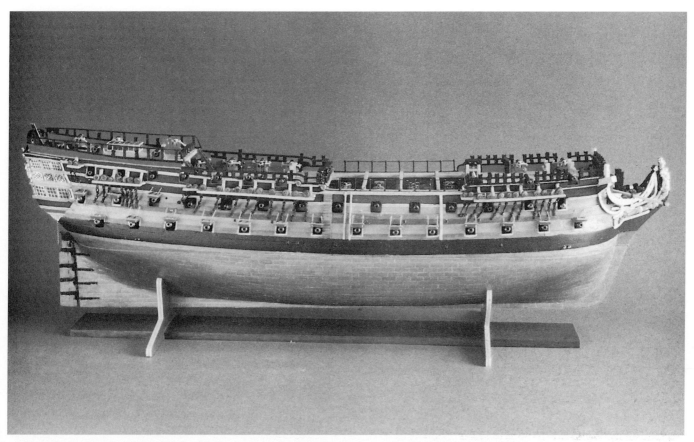

Fig. 1.23  If you don't have much display space available, the project could finish at this stage.

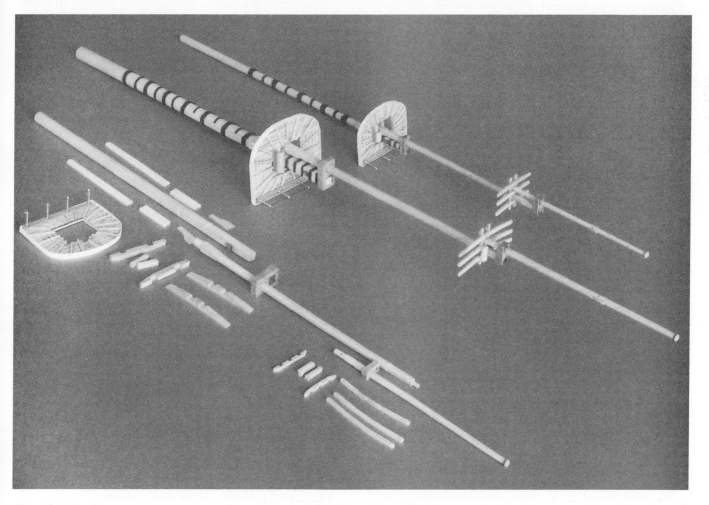

Fig. 1.24  The foremast components with main and mizen masts asssembled.

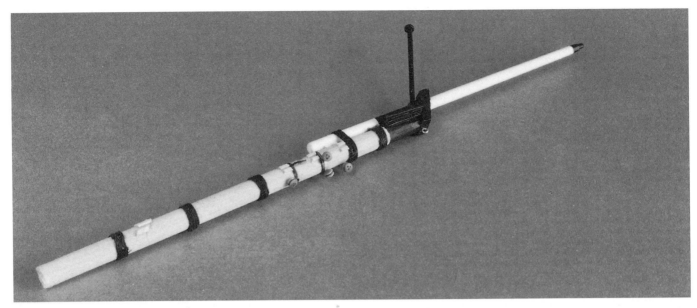

**Fig. 1.25 The bowsprit assembly.**

ter deck. Deck gratings and gun carriages were made, painted and fitted (without barrels), together with the beams to support the quarter deck. The bitts fore and aft of the main mast also serve as supports for the deck above and so it was found advantageous to fit the beams first then, with a straight edge across the tops of the beams, establish the height for the posts on the bitts before dowelling them in position, (**Fig.1.15**).

Planking the quarter deck, poop deck and forecastle deck followed the same procedure as previously used for the main deck.

There were two, what Corel call fillers for the cabin fascia under the poop deck. It was essential to check the size of these with the appropriate photo-etched brass pieces before fitting.

It certainly would not have been a very nice job to do later.

Similarly, it saved a bit of anguish by pre-painting red, the strip used for lining the inside of the bulwarks. It ensured a neat and clean-cut line between lining and the waterways.

The bulwark capping strips for the forecastle deck needed to be made from something a bit wider than 5mm due to the lateral curve involved. I had a check through the parts list and found that, with care, I could shape them from the 10 x 1mm beech provided. Alternatively, I could have scarfed two pieces of 5 x 1mm edgewise to achieve the same result. Careful rubbing down followed by a coat of sanding sealer prepared these items for painting and avoided evidence of the rather course grain.

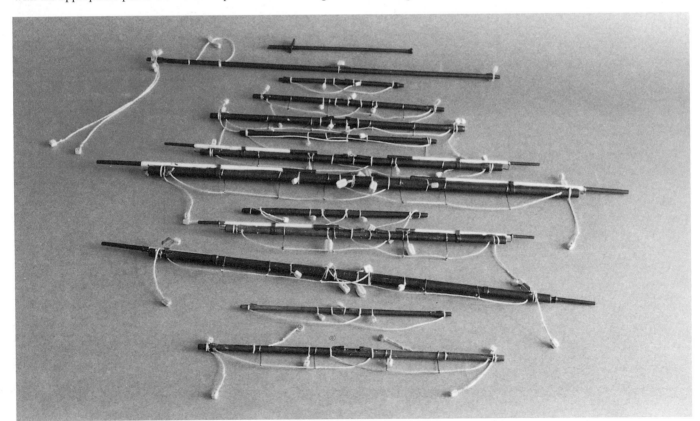

**Fig. 1.26 The yards with blocks and footropes attached.**

Fig. 1.27 Ready to commence rigging.

**Fig. 1.28  Bowsprit shrouds and bobstays.**

**Fig. 1.29  Burton pendants and associated tackle.**

The deck fittings, skylight, gratings, etc., all followed the usual kit procedures but, unfortunately, because of the 1/100 scale, the selection of beech as the prime material proved a little difficult. Making small parts would have been easier using a finer grained or more dense timber. It was, therefore, essential to ensure that all cutting tools were absolutely sharp and that no undue pressure was exerted on the smaller sections of strip material if flaking of edges and corners was to be avoided. Even when sanding, sharp corners could suddenly disappear.

**Figs. 1.16 & 1.17** show the major deck fittings in place and **Fig.1.18** shows the model, thus far, mounted on the stand.

The fabrication of the belfry roof at first looked a bit unwieldy, again bearing in mind the selection of beech. However, I have to say that it actually worked out quite well, although I would have anticipated that this would have been a part considered for casting.

## Finishing the Hull Exterior

The cheek plates above and below the hawse hole area and on up the sides of the stem were the first items fitted, **(Fig.1.19)**. The flexible beech strip provided made the curving of the pieces very easy.

The head timbers and rails were more of a problem. The instructions recommended that the assembly be joined "preventively" without glue and offered up against the hull, making such adjustments as necessary until an acceptable fit was attained. Bearing in mind the size of the parts and the nature of the timber, this seemed to me to be a very optimistic proposition. I found the whole structure more easily put together by making

Fig. 1.30 The caparthins and futtock shrouds on the main mast.

Fig. 1.31 Shrouds and ratlines with backstays rigged on stools.

**Fig. 1.32 Crowsfeet rigged from stay to top with euphroe tackle. The stays and preventers are rigged with hearts and staked together.**

the first head-rail the key to the assembly, again see **Fig.1.19**.

I cut and tapered two pieces of 4 x 2mm flexi-strip and soaked them for about twenty minutes remembering that they were to be bent edgewise. Each strip was then bent to the true shape of the rails shown on the drawings. It was quite amazing how well the strip bent around such tight curves. In order to retain the correct shape the part was then pinned to my work board. The second strip was immediately bent and pinned on top of the first to ensure that both pieces were identical in shape. They were left overnight to thoroughly dry out. When released from the jig the following morning, the shape was permanent and both pieces identical. Having been bent in the "flat" it was easy to fix them in position from hull to stem.

The head timbers were then made up to rough shape and individually fitted between the first head-rail and the stem.

Unexpectedly, I found that the more difficult feature was the grating deck that fitted between the upper head-rails. Certainly, as instructed, it was necessary to make a cardboard template to get the shape right. When constructing the inset deck, the frame members were left a little on the full side on length. However, it was deemed unwise to leave too much because trimming such a flimsy structure was always going to be a bit hazardous. The assembly was gradually built up, frame member and gratings together. The basic outline was trimmed to the template and final fitting to the top head-rails carried out very gently. The seats of ease and the knightheads were then made and fitted.

Some painting needed to be done as the assembly of these various items proceeded, particularly on the roundhouses and facing to the forecastle deck, which could have got a bit tricky if left

until later. The rails assembly, together with the roundhouses and seats of ease, are to be seen in **Figs. 1.20 & 1.21**.

The fenders and exterior steps were added next before proceeding to the building up of the quarter galleries and stern assembly. I cannot emphasise too much, how important it was to study the drawings and instructions at this stage, before working on the stern area, probably the most demanding part of the project in terms of craftsmanship and ingenuity. The mixture of woodwork and brasswork needed to be carefully put together in order to reap the benefit of the photo-etched brass parts. Sizing the brass parts and trimming off the tabs is most important before finally fixing pieces permanently in place. Again, some of the instructions were a bit optimistic, like trying to bend 1 x 1mm strip over a 4.5mm radius to make the mouldings over two of the stern windows! Painting at intermediate stages obviated awkward brushwork later on. Cyanoacrylate and two-part epoxy adhesives were the adhesives used throughout this part of the build. The finished construction of the stern area is shown in **Fig.1.22**.

The timber heads and bulwark rails presented a few problems in that the timbers were 3mm lengths of 3 x 2mm strip. Getting the ends perfectly square to make a good glue joint on the end grain to the tops of the bulwarks was never going to be very successful, even with the help of a mini bench sander, not a piece of kit to be found in many beginners' tool boxes. I decided to let the grain run the other way, i.e.; fore and aft, cyanoacrylate the "side" of the strip to the bulwark rail and, when properly cured, used a sharp scalpel to pare the tapered sides across the end grain. The top was indented with a round file. However, it was essential to make sound glued joints to avoid the heads being knocked off.

Fig. 1.33 The model with standing rigging completed.

**Fig. 1.34  The bowsprit running rigging.**

The poop deck rails and supports made from 2 x 1mm and 2 x 2mm respectively, were also going to be vulnerable items. The strongest way that I found was to drill 2.5mm dia. holes into the deck sides and gently push the supports into position without glue. The height of the rail was then marked and trimmed to size before finally gluing the joints at deck level. It was not necessary to worry about the 2mm square peg in the 2.5mm dia. hole, the gap made the ideal space for the glue! It was just required to drill the holes truly in line, remembering that the widths of both rail and supports were the same.

One deviation from the advised sequence that I did make was the assembly of the chain plates. The reason that I did this was because I wanted to photograph the model in a hull-complete state before I proceeded to completion. Some model makers with limited display space may find this stage of construction as an acceptable completion of the model.

I found the drawings and instructions somewhat lacking with regard to the small deadeye assemblies on the channels, with little detail of what the linkages should look like. There is a very brief note in the instructions, but hardly adequate for any but the more experienced modeller. The collars for the deadeyes were as provided, but the links below were made up from brass wire - a suitable length with an eye formed at each

end and shorter than the links provided for the 5mm dia. main shroud items.

The guns were quite straightforward to make up, although at this scale, the average model maker would find it very fiddly to fully rig them. In fact, I would go as far as to say they would not look right and the model would become overcluttered. I contented myself with just adding the breeching rope. Again some inadequacy in the documentation was experienced, this time with a lack of clear detail regarding the carronades on the poop deck.

The completed hull-only model for limited space display is depicted in **Fig.1.23**.

## The Masts and Spars

Upper masts usually have a square-sectioned heel and many spars have an octagonal centre section. Here, we have a kit which, for once, has got it right and specifies square -sectioned timber for those items. It just makes spinning the parts a little more difficult if your turning facility only features a three-jaw self-centering chuck. Again, the wood provided was beech and I'm not too sure that that is the ideal. I can envisage that in time, given the wrong display conditions, some distortion might occur.

Fig. 1.35  Fore yard rigging with tack, sheet and clue garnet.

Fig. 1.36  The main yard lift with topsail clue line and sheet.

**Fig. 1.37 The main topsail yard lift shackled to the topgallant clue line.**

The making of the mast parts was not difficult, but it was essential as always, to keep tools razor sharp to accurately cut the joints for the cross trees and trestle trees.

Mast caps needed some rather delicate attention to open out some of the holes; too much force and you have a cap in two pieces. A further point about the caps; they had to be assembled to their respective upper mast before putting the top above in place! The rake of the mast had to be taken into consideration when assembling the trestle trees, cross trees and tops remembering that the surface of the tops had to be parallel to the waterline.

Apart from the base of the lower top platforms and the rail stanchions, all parts had to be fabricated and jointed and so making the masts was something more than a weekend job.

Woldings were wound with thread - a starting loop, then five turns round the mast, through the loop then pulled under the windings. A touch of cyanoacrylate prepared the excess thread for close trimming. The mast bands were simulated using black card cut into the appropriate width strips. I selected card that was black right through its thickness rather than just surface coloured the latter would require painting!

The masts were left in natural wood apart from the doublings, trees and tops which were painted matt black, (**Fig.1.24**). The bowsprit is shown in **Fig.1.25**.

Many of the spars, as mentioned above, were made from square-sectioned wood. Each spar was tapered on the square in the usual fashion, then the corners taken off to make an octagonal section throughout its length. The length of the centre portion was marked and the outer parts further filed to a basic round section. The spar could then be held lightly on one circular section so that the other could be spun-finished (**Fig.1.26**).

It was helpful to attach all blocks, footropes and stirrups before putting the spars up on to the masts. However, having followed the recommended sequence, this got done anyway. The model, ready to start the standing rigging, is pictured in **Fig.1.27**.

## The Standing Rigging

Four sizes of thread were provided in the kit but, unfortunately, all tan-coloured. This would be considered a major problem if, as I did, you wished to make the standing rigging either black, or very dark brown, to give that permanent tarred effect. It meant either a messy dye job or replacing the thread where necessary.

It was fortunate that I spotted one other problem before starting. Records show that the main and fore shrouds on *Bellona* were 11in rope. This, of course, refers to the circumference and relates to a diameter of 3.5in which, at 1/100 scale is 0.035in or 0.89mm. The instruction manual specifies 1.2mm diameter which is, and looks, grossly oversize. Depending on your own particular cutting and rigging techniques, you could finish up with surplus 1.2mm thread but insufficient 0.8mm, the nearest correct size in the kit. I took the easy way out and found some black thread of suitable diameter to use on the shrouds. Incidently, the manual indicates oversize material for all shrouds. It is a factor that should be taken into consideration if you don't want the result to be top heavy - not an uncommon fault in period ship models.

It was worth remembering to drill through blocks and deadeyes as necessary to ensure a clear passage for the relevant cordage. A further aid to swift threading is to stiffen the leading end of each line with a dab of cyanoacrylate - a sort of built-in bodkin.

The rigging diagrams were found to be excellent in terms of sequence of fitting and, when used in conjunction with the "Rigging Course" given in the instruction manual, this part of the project was as straightforward as one could expect with this amount of detail and at this scale. I don't think that I can add much that would be of significant help, apart from perhaps reminding model makers to remove rings and watches, before starting any rigging session.

One technical aspect that worried me a little was the rigging of the topgallant shrouds. I would have anticipated that the shroud would have started at the top of the topgallant mast, passed through the crosstrees and then have terminated at the sheerpole on the topmast shroud below. The drawings showed that it continued down to the lower deadeyes on the top below, a feature which I would have thought came in somewhat later in history. However, Corel have obviously done a good research job on this kit and I acknowledge that pinpointing introductory dates for changes in the rigging of such vessels is extremely difficult. My own research has not been conclusive.

The rigging process itself starts with the bowsprit bobstays and shrouds, the latter being tightened up with lanyards and deadeyes, (**Fig.1.28**). Then Burton pendants were rigged, it not being often that these features are included on a model. Sometimes referred to as mast tackles or side tackles, they were used to install or tighten shrouds, fish anchors or moving heavy loads and boats, (**Fig.1.29**). The pendants proper were attached to the mast in the same way as the shrouds but went on first. The associated tackle fitted to the pendants and to eyebolts on the channels by means of hooks.

The sequence of applying the shrouds to the mastheads is clearly and diagrammatically explained on the drawings. The usual care not to over tension was observed, the same precaution being taken when rigging the catharpins, (**Fig.1.30**). The aim was just to get some tension in them and not distort the shrouds.

When rigging the futtock shrouds, again **Fig.1.30**, the same care with tension needed to be applied so as not to pull the lower shrouds out of line. I usually put a dob of epoxy to the bottom of the deadeye assembly to stick it firmly to the upper surface of the top. This took the strain when tensioning the upper shrouds, avoiding the pull going down through the system to the shrouds below.

The ratlines, **Fig.1.31**, as always, were tedious in their application. In this instance, the small scale brought them closer together and it was most helpful on the eyes to place a piece of card or folded plain paper between the mast and the inside of the shrouds as a background while tying on each flight. Buff or other pale colour is preferable to soften the contrast with the black thread, but white is better than nothing. Incidently, you may find, as I did, that the ratlines can be applied in, say, six stages. Each stage completed one side of one mast and, between stages, I rigged the fore and aft stays. This tended to break up the tedium and prevented a degree of strain on the eyes.

Note that the fore stay and main stay were of 17in and 18in rope respectively, which translates back to 1.4mm and 1.5mm diameter.

It was suggested in the manual that the euphroe blocks, used to rig the crowsfeet, be made by modifying 8mm x two-hole violin blocks. Strictly speaking, the euphroe should have a row of holes numbering half those that are in the fore edge of the relevant top. Obviously this was not possible with the violin block modification but, with care, and selection of the right block, it would be possible to drill two extra holes. However, it was not too difficult to fabricate a euphroe from scrap to contain even more holes. The length of each block was very slightly over-scale, but it did avoid the unsightly bunching and misalignment of the crowsfeet at the point where they passed through the euphroe. The crowsfeet are shown in **Fig.1.32**.

The backstays were then set up to complete the standing rigging, again see **Fig.1.31**.

The model, with standing rigging completed, can be seen in **Fig.1.33**.

## The Running Rigging

Again, the numerical sequence of assembly shown in the manual was followed without mishap. Information on belaying points was scattered about, some on drawings, and some needing to be gleaned from the rigging list in the manual. To be fair, most of the information was there, it just needed a bit of finding. One feature that should not be overlooked, and one not mentioned in the manual, is what happens to the excess thread after it has been belayed at the appropriate point. There are two ways to terminate the rigging. If a belaying pin is involved, then I would normally trim the thread close to the pin and then hang a hank of separately-coiled thread from the top of the pin. Rigging that is tied off at a rail, bitt or lower ratline, I take on down to the deck below before trimming to length. The trimmed end is then hidden by a separately-wound coil laying flat on the deck.

All running rigging was done using the tan-coloured thread provided.

## Finishing Off

Anchors were rigged, the ensign staff erected and lanterns mounted to finish off the model. A general overview of the model was essential to ensure that no significant detail had been missed. A worthwhile practice, if you possess an SLR camera, is to attach a close-up facility and view various parts of the model through the view finder. It is surprising just what can come to light using such a concentrated field of view, untrimmed ends of rigging, trimmed ends lurking under gun carriages or even missed areas of paintwork!

I deliberately left the flags off because I couldn't get them to look right. I practised on a spare piece of the flag sheet provided, but found it too stiff and inflexible to attain a natural-looking drape. My lack of expertise in this respect decided me that the model would not be enhanced by poorly-flown flags. However, anyone also coming to the same decision, should not forget to rig the relevant flag halliards.

Further details of the running rigging and finished model are shown in **Figs. 1.34 to 1.37**.

## Conclusions

In spite of the fact that Corel mentioned less-experienced modellers in their manual, it is my opinion that the kit is not one to be recommended for those who have not previously made several fairly complex models.

The beech material was excellent in itself but, I felt, a better choice could have been made for the yards and some of the smaller items that had to be fabricated. No black thread for the standing rigging was a disappointment in a kit of this class.

The colour guide would be improved if based on item number priority, rather than colour priority, even perhaps becoming part of the parts list proper. The parts list would also have been enhanced if the total quantity of each item needed, either provided in the kit or to be fabricated, had been indicated.

The research that went into this kit was excellent and certainly more extensive than usual, providing for a very nice model indeed. The questionable size of cordage for the shrouds was therefore somewhat surprising.

The drawings themselves were excellent and, although a few more finer details of the running rigging would have been welcomed, on the whole as good as I've seen in a kit to date and would be more than adequate for anyone enterprising enough to build a *Bellona* to a larger scale. The materials were generally of good quality as were the pre-made fittings, although there were only just enough. A tidy and disciplined bench was therefore essential to avoid loss.

Worth building? Yes, most definitely, but don't expect a quick or easy passage to the end result, in fact quite a tour de force. This was not a throw-together kit and there was a very considerable amount of patient work to do.

Good value? Yes, but be prepared to buy that black thread if you don't want a messy dye job. Certainly it is on the cards to achieve an exhibition standard model.

The kit is distributed by Euro Models, 35 Crown Road, St.Margaret's, Twickenham, TW1 3EJ and retails at just under £200.

## References

"*The 74-gun ship Bellona*" by Brian Lavery, published by Conway Maritime Press ISBN 0 85177 368 0.

"*The Masting and Rigging of English Ships of War*" by James Lees, published by Conway Maritime Press ISBN 0 85177 290 0.

# CHAPTER 2

# H.M.S. *UNICORN*

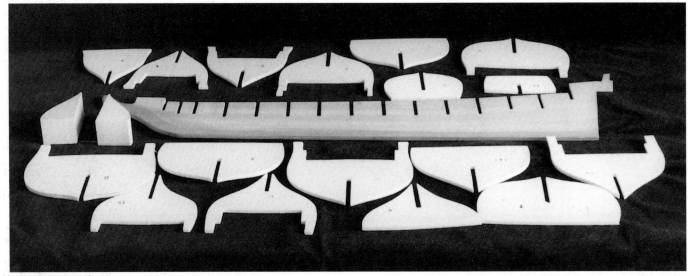

**Fig. 2.1 The frames and false keel. Note the keel has been edged and varnished.**

The *Unicorn* was a copy of the captured French privateer Tygre. The dockyards were instructed to precisely take off lines of the Tygre and record details of dimensions, fastenings, yards and masts. It is most likely that, with pressure from Admiral George Anson for a new and better all-weather cruiser, the design of the *Unicorn* fell, where necessary, outside the confines of the Establishment type.

Chapman, in his "Architectura Navalis Mercatoria" (1768), used a Navy Board original as a basis for his illustration of *Unicorn* as the British example of a fast sailing warship.

Launched at Plymouth in 1748 as a 24-gun frigate, it was modified in 1756 to add four carriage guns to the quarterdeck, thus converting the vessel to a 28-gun frigate. *Unicorn* was broken up at Sheerness in 1771.

There are a couple of features in the kit design which I feel should be called into question. Certainly the date 1790, is incorrect as is the statement that it was designed by Chapman. There is no doubt that the model is of the 1748 vessel, the kit provides for the correct two window quarter-lights and the correct beakhead style bows. (Its sister ship, Lyme, had rounded bows.) Although *Unicorn* carried a main battery of 24 guns, there were, in fact, thirteen ports each side. I have assumed that in the usual manner, there was not a gun position forward of the foremast, although I have chosen to put in the extra port. The kit provides for eight guns on the quarterdeck, but again, I left four of these out and made the model as per the 1756 modification, albeit that the quarterdeck guns were lighter than those in the main battery.

## The Kit

This is a very well-presented kit. A plan pack includes three sheets of full size views of the model, these being supported by a further seven sheets of constructional detail sketches. While these are all well-draughted, I did find one or two confusing differences between sketches and drawings.

The materials sand fittings were all of very good quality. The strip material was of a particularly high standard and the kit contained a wealth of pre-cut parts.

The stern ornamentation and quarter galleries, made from ply in earlier versions of the kit, now come as soft metal castings with very crisp detailing.

The model finishes up at 840mm long and 730mm high.

## Tools Required

Apart from the very basic model maker's tool kit, a 12 volt high speed drill is almost an essential and a similarly-powered disc sander also makes life a lot easier. You also need a couple of sharp chisels to honk off the surplus material from the bow blocks. A small plane and a flat cabinet maker's scraper for plank finishing take a lot of the hard work out of this otherwise dusty task.

Paint is required for the stern decoration, either oil-based enamels or acrylics are OK. Either satin or matt varnish will be useful to seal the hull surfaces.

White PVA, cyanoacrylate and two part epoxy adhesives are necessary to put everything together.

Dye, either black or very dark brown, is required to colour some of the thread for the standing rigging.

## Building the Hull Carcase

The basic hull construction is in the conventional bulkheads on false keel format, these parts coming already cut to profile, (**Fig.2. 1**). However, a little bit of work was needed to be done to them in order to get the assembly as it should be. There was a number of additional little things that I wanted to do over and above the items shown in the construction manual to improve the standard of the model.

First, the false keel, being made of ply had an exposed edge which I certainly did not want to be in evidence on the finished job. Not being sure at this stage whether or not there would be enough material in the kit, I raided my scrap box for a strip of 5 x 0.5mm and edged the keel before I started to do anything else. If you have ever got fingermarks on the stem and keel and found them awkward to remove after you have done the planking, you will appreciate why I also sanded and matt varnished those areas at this time, (again **Fig.2.1**).

I then made sure that the false keel was absolutely flat and straight before assembling the frames. It is easier to take any corrective action at this stage rather than after the frames have

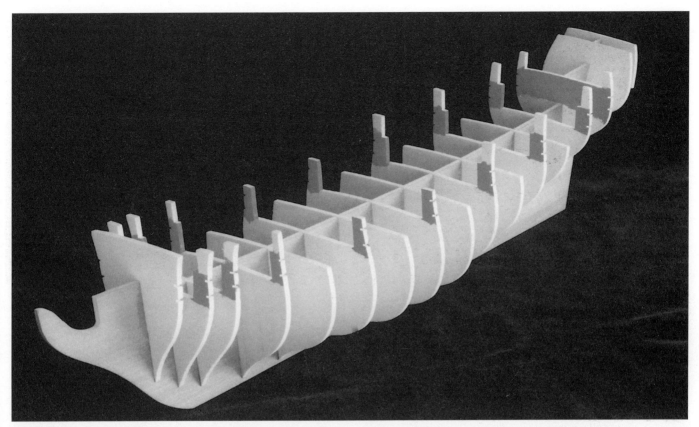

**Fig. 2.2 The assembled frames and keel. The exposed surfaces within the gun deck have been painted dark red.**

been assembled. The slots in the keel, bulkheads and decks needed a little easing and, more importantly, deepening to ensure that the level of the gun-deck on the relevant bulkheads coincided with the top edge of the false keel. These were fixed first, using a square to get them into true alignment. It was also important to ensure that the tops of the first four bulkheads were in line. The three bulkheads at the stern, also have to coincide with the local levels of the false keel, but with allowance to file the top edges of the bulkheads to provide a flat angular seating for the deck pieces at these points. Before the adhesive set, I used the gun-deck as a jig, dry-fitted, to hold everything in place while the glue finished curing overnight. The resultant assembly is shown in **Fig.2.2**.

The blocks each side of the keel at the bows were then offered up and the outline of the first frame traced on to the block's rear face. The curved line of the stem was marked on to the adjacent face and all the surplus material removed before gluing the blocks in place. The pre-shaped piece for the stern, provided in the kit, was also fitted at this stage. The blocks and edges of the frames were then trimmed and sanded to provide the required seating for the first planking, using a planking strip to constantly monitor the shape throughout the length of the hull.

Having read through the instructions before I started, I realised that once the upper deck had been assembled, it would not be possible to do any work on the gun-deck. Accordingly, I chose to paint the bulkheads on their inner, fore and aft faces with dark red paint. These will be seen to some degree either through the opening in the upper deck or the gun-ports, and I did not want to see the bare edges or exposed faces of plywood on the finished job. The areas painted were those between the gun-deck and upper deck.

The gun-deck was the next feature to be tackled. The

instructions indicated that this should be fitted in place, then planked. You may find it easier, as I did, to plank the deck before fitting. If you are going to plank the deck using the three butt-shift method, working on the bench before assembly permits better access and a more stable working platform, thus helping to keep the butts in true alignment.

Corel suggest that the edges of each plank should be blackened with a pencil before gluing in place. I used a 4B grade of pencil and found that this method worked very well, providing a fine and subtle lining that was just about right for this scale. It is so easy to overdo the caulking effect and spoil the whole issue. The entire surface of the false deck was planked, the locating slots being cut away after the deck surface had been scraped and smoothed ready for assembly. Before committing the glue pot, another check was made to ensure that all the deck seating surfaces were clean and in correct alignment. The deck was then glued and pinned in place.

## The First Planking

The first planks to be fitted were those that defined the top and bottom surfaces of the gun-ports, (**Fig.2.3**). Rather than totally rely on the pre-cut notches in the edges of the frames, I decided to make up one gun carriage in order to establish the actual height of the barrel from the deck. This height was then marked on the edge of the frames together with a second and third mark 5mm above and below the first. For the most part these marks coincided with the notches, although there were one or two where there was a bit of deviation.

Having fixed the two subject planks each side, the side of the gun-ports were then delineated by short lengths of planking strip applied to the inner faces of the longitudinal planks, (Fig.2.4). It is important to recognise that these short lengths

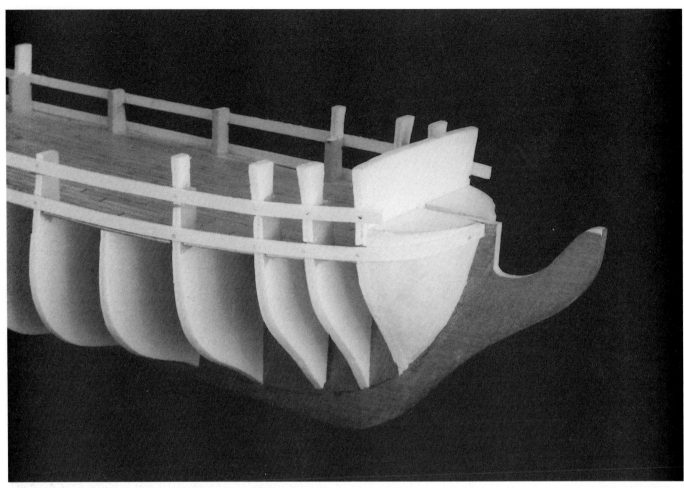

Fig. 2.3 The first two planking strips at top and bottom of the gun ports.

Fig. 2.4 The sides of the gun ports outlined.

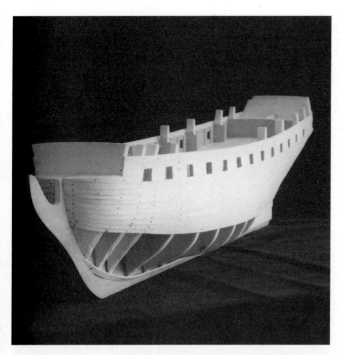

**Fig. 2.5 The first planking on its way down to the keel.**

matching to the sides of the short uprights previously fitted. The remainder of the hull was planked in the usual manner down to the keel, (**Fig.2.5**). Below the line of the gun-ports, I found that each plank needed tapering at each end to about half width over a length of 160mm. This will vary a bit, I guess, according to how you trimmed and shaped the edges of the frames. There were still some places, of course, where stealers needed to be fitted. Some bending was required at the front end, but this was easily accomplished with the aid of a plank nipper.

There is a chain dotted line shown at the stern of the side elevation drawing which is most confusing. It is not apparent from any other view or sketch as to what it represents and I certainly could not find reference to it in the English version of the instructions. I mention it only because I ignored it and did not run into any subsequent difficulty!

The first planking was scraped and sanded to get to an even surface all over. Absolute smoothness was not essential; in fact, a slight roughness provided an ideal key for the contact adhesive I proposed to use for the second planking.

## The Second Planking

As with the first layer, the second planking was started at the line of the gun-ports. Reference to the drawings and the material list is essential to make sure that the right size and colour of timber is used, (**Fig.2.6**). Having laid two rows of planking below the ports, one black and one light strip, the main wale was then applied. A fairly severe bend

be vertical and parallel to the frames. They should not be square to the deck and they should not be square to the keel. This will become obvious if you remember that gun-ports were essentially spaces between actual frames.

The first planking then continued, filling in the spaces between the gun-ports. The pieces were left overlong for later

**Fig. 2.6 The second planking starts at the gun ports using differently coloured strips. The wales are then added before planking down to the keel.**

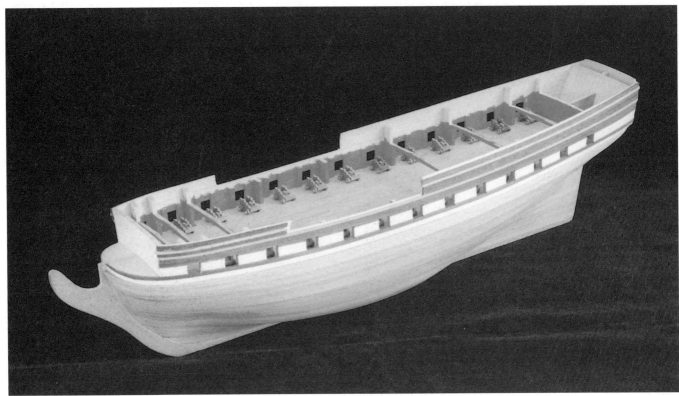

Fig. 2.7 The completion of the planking with gun ports sized and the main battery in place.

Fig. 2.8 The upper deck in place. The bulwark edges have been shaped to take the decorative pieces.

**Fig 2.9 The decorative pieces in place in the rough.**

at the bows requires the strips to be soaked in very hot water for a while to get the fibres nice and pliable. A couple of minutes stuck down the spout of my electric kettle proved to be just right.

The rest of the planking down to the keel could now be fixed, the planks needing to be tapered as for the first planking. However, don't expect to follow exactly the same lines as before. Although the width of planking is the same, the thickness is less and thus cannot sustain any tendency to sideways bending or twisting. It is most important that this is recognised, because with the use of contact adhesive, the entire area of the plank must sit flat down on the surface of the first planking. If it doesn't, you get a buckling effect at one edge of the plank where it lifts off. Total disaster!

Bending the planks around the bows was carefully done with a plank nipper. With thinner planking, you just don't have to squeeze too hard. If you do, you are liable to see the marks on the outer surface when you finally sand down the hull.

The planking above the line of the gun-ports was then put on. The gun-ports were then sized, trimming the ends of the intermediate planks to attain correct width and cutting into the top and bottom black strips where necessary to get the right height. Note that the top and bottom edges of the ports should be square to the sides. I made up an 11mm square plug gauge to ensure that they were all the same size. The hull at this stage is shown in **Fig.2.7**.

## Completing the Hull Structure

Before assembling the upper deck, the gun carriages have to be made and positioned, but without the barrels. The latter are put in place later from the outside of the hull. It is therefore imperative to establish the right position for each carriage so that when assembled, all the barrels protrude through the hull the same distance. The easiest way is to determine that position with one carriage, fix it in place, then measure the gap between the front of the carriage and the inside of the hull. A "feeler" was made to this dimension and used to ensure that all the carriages were positioned identically.

The instructions suggest that the protruding part of the frames be cut off after assembling the upper deck. I chose to cut them off prior to this operation, leaving just enough to locate the deck. This enabled the deck to be planked on the bench in the same way as the gun-deck. The insides of the bulwarks were planked after putting the deck in place, **(Fig.2.8)**.

At this juncture, you may wish to drill holes in the gun-deck for the masts - see my later notes under the heading Masts and Yards.

The bulwark rails and the decorating pieces were made and fitted at the same time. The decorative parts were made up from short lengths of dowel rod but, instead of leaving them plain as depicted in the constructional sketches, I drilled them through with a 3mm diameter drill, countersunk the outer face and glued in a piece of lighter shade dowel material, **(Fig.2.9)**. A fair amount of trimming and subsequent "offering up" is

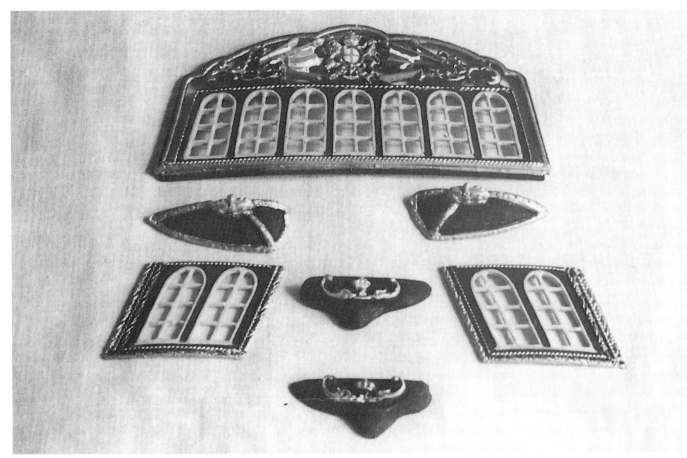

**Fig 2.10 The stern decoration parts.**

**Fig 2.11 The glazing strips in place**

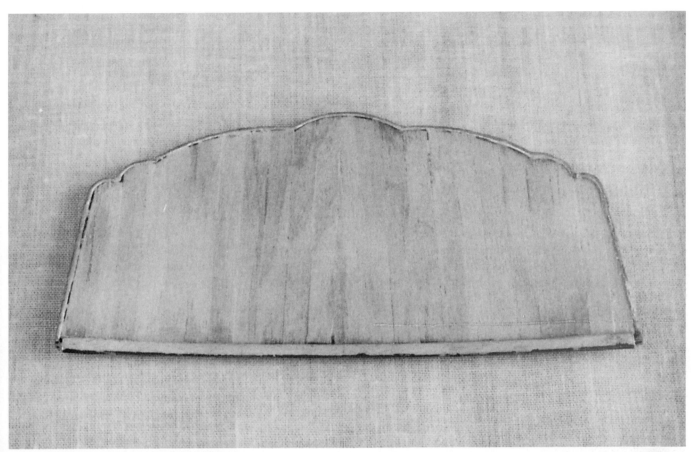

**Fig 2.12 The transom vertically planked.**

required to get everything looking shipshape.

The rails amidships are shown at one-plank-width height above deck on the constructional sketch but flush with the deck on the main drawing. In my case the drawing won, mainly because it better suited the diameters of the decorative dowels and the thickness of the rails themselves. The rails toward the stern can be bent to profile relatively easily. However, those at the forecastle cannot and probably the best way to handle these is to glue two pieces of suitable length edge to edge and cut the inner and outer curves from the resultant shape.

The hull was given a coat of acrylic matt varnish at this stage and allowed to dry while I built the stand provided in the kit.

## The Stern Decoration

Before assembling the several cast metal parts associated with the decoration, the last frame surface was curved as required. The instructions advise that this curved surface be faced with vertical planking strips. However, I am sure that you will find, as I did, that this is not the best way of attaining the planked effect visible through the stern casting.

I first gave all the castings a priming coat of acrylic paint, white at all window frames and black everywhere else. When thoroughly dry, the frames were painted pale yellow, the draped flags picked out in the various specified colours and the giltwork dry brushed with gold, (**Fig.2.10**).

The glazing strips were then carefully glued on to the back of the castings, (**Fig.2.11**) and then, the recessed back of the stern panel was planked in with vertical planking strips, (**Fig.2.12**). This panel was then gently bent to conform to the

curve on the rear frame of the hull and glued in place, making sure that the painted casting was protected from finger marks by wearing a pair of thin film disposable kitchen mitts.

The pre-shaped top and bottom pieces to the quarter galleries were then positioned and glued, (**Fig.2.13**). The side castings were then bent to sit against the inside rear of the back casting with the front edge adjusted to follow the profile

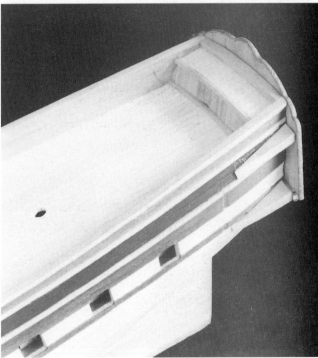

**Fig 2.13 Preparation for the stern galleries.**

of the hull. Two-part epoxy adhesive was used to fix these pieces into place. The two crowned top castings were then assembled.

The castings on the underside of the galleries needed considerable adjustment to their rear and top surfaces to attain the best fit. The degree of adjustment largely depends on the actual shape that has been produced at this particular part of the hull when doing the second planking. Unfortunately, the view of the stern and the side elevation on the drawing are a little at odds with one another when it comes to showing the position of these lower castings. What you get and what you see aren't entirely identical either.

After I had got all the parts assembled on the hull to my satisfaction, (**Fig.2.14**), I felt that the window frames, being totally in yellow, did not look right. I therefore painted the edges of the frames white, with just a faint tinge of yellow mixed in. The effect was much more acceptable.

By chance at this juncture, I was having a look at some of the fittings and realised that the figurehead casting was a fairly solid piece of metal and would not easily be slotted to fit over the thickness of the stem. I therefore decided to cut the relevant shape into the stem at this point, (**Fig.2.15**), rather than leave it until later when, perhaps, things would be a bit more hazardous.

## Finishing the Hull Details

This part of the building process comprises the channels, the upper deck ports, the head-rails and the making and assembling of the general deck fittings. The instructions advise that these items should be tackled in numerical order. However, my advice is that you read about what has to be done in total and then select a sequence that suits your own way of working. I say this because one of the recommended earlier tasks is the fitting of the channels. These are edge fitting and, therefore, are a bit vulnerable if you like to work with the hull resting on your lap. I chose to fit the upper deck gun-ports first.

Some considerable thought was given to this task in order that as clean a hole as possible was introduced through the bulwarks. It was obvious from the word go that you can't simply drill a 9mm hole straight through; in fact if you try to drill such a hole at all, you will undoubtedly split the inner planking as the drill exits. I actually made up a sample assembly to try various ideas and found that the following procedure proved to be the most successful.

Having first marked the correct position for each port, I then cut and removed the portion of upper rail at those points to match the diameter of the turned brass inserts provided in the kit. A series of 2mm dia. holes was then drilled around a 7mm dia. circle and the centre portion pushed out. The residue was then carefully cut and filed until a push fit for the brass insert was attained. The insert was introduced from inside the bulwarks and pressed home with a piece of scrap timber just using finger pressure. This sequence is shown in **Fig.2.16**.

## The Deck Fittings

The various deck fittings, skylight and hatches were then made up and placed in position, (**Fig.2.17**). With regard to the gratings, I found it easier to assemble the grating pieces, trim the edges and frame them with the coamings before assembly to the deck, (**Fig.2.18**).

The pin racks, chimney and other fittings, (**Fig.2.19**), were drilled, dowelled and glued to the deck for total security. For dowels, I cut the heads off of some brass pins and drilled the bottom surfaces of the relevant fittings to provide a press fit. Similar size holes were then drilled in the appropriate deck positions and cyanoacrylate used as an adhesive. The important factor here, is to select the right size drill, in order to attain the press fit which needs to be as tight as that can be assembled with firm finger pressure. Remember that the bitts and pin racks, in particular, have to take quite a bit of "pull" when it comes to rigging the vessel later on.

A further point of accuracy concerns the chimney. The

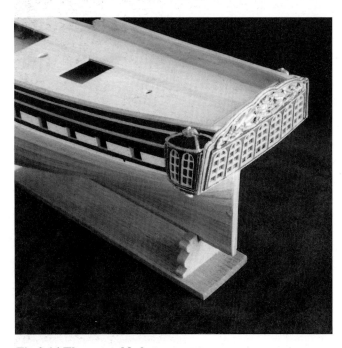

**Fig 2.14 The assembled stern parts.**

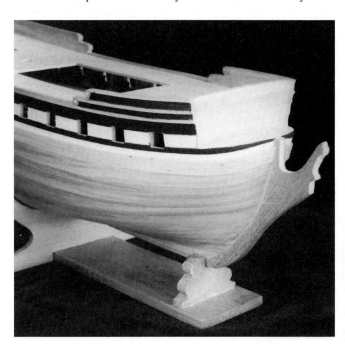

**Fig 2.15 The stem cut to house the figurehead.**

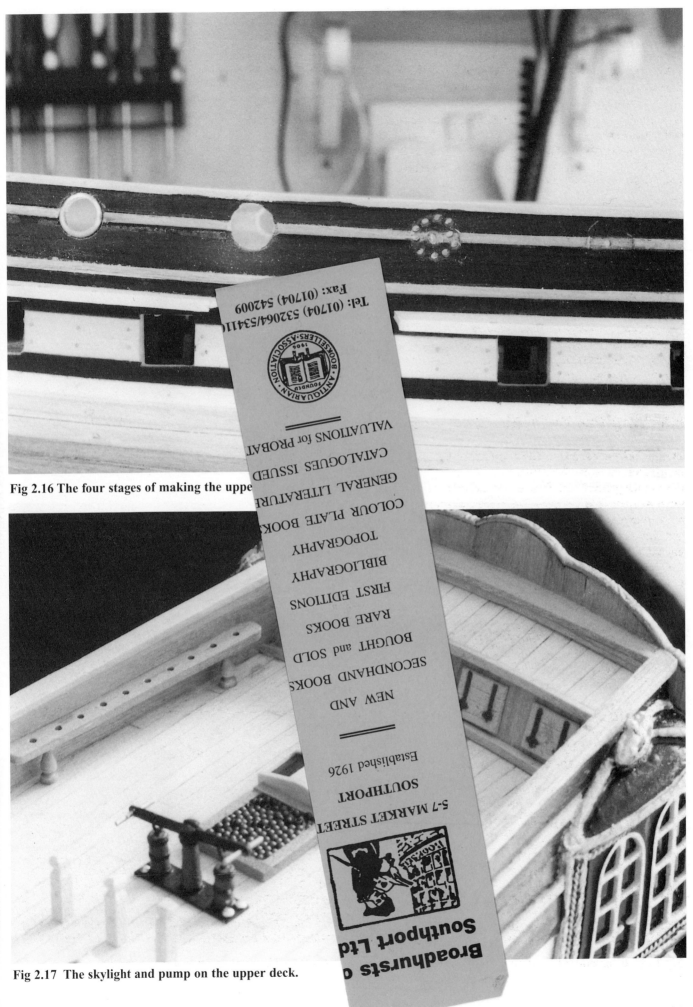

Fig 2.16 The four stages of making the uppe...

Fig 2.17 The skylight and pump on the upper deck.

Fig 2.18 An assembled grating, capstan and ship's wheel in place.

Fig 2.19 Pin racks and bitts glued and dowelled.

Fig 2.20  Modified steps down to the gun deck.

drawings indicate that this should be 20mm high above the surface of the fore-deck. It would also continue down through the gun-deck to the galley below. Thus the chimney was made long enough to pass through the fore-deck and be dowelled to the surface of the gun-deck. Just a small point maybe, but the stack can just be seen by prying eyes looking forward into the well of the deck.

The steps from the upper deck down to the gun deck should be wider than the treads provided in the kit. A simple scrap strip replacement can be fitted (**Fig.2.20**).

## The Head Timbers and Rails

The base structure was found to be relatively straightforward to make, although it has to be said that it needs very accurate cutting to ensure that all the joints are strong and secure. This particularly applies to the three angular supports each side between the prow and the upper frame. I found that epoxy

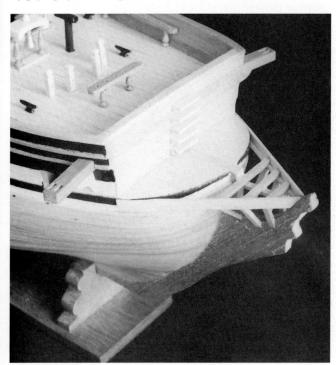

Fig 2.21  The head timbers base structure.

Fig 2.22 The completed front end. Note two slots for the gammoning.

**Fig 2.23 The completed hull and stand.**

adhesive was best since it allowed time to get everything truly aligned before it "grabbed". PVA didn't have enough initial stickiness and cyanoacrylate was too quick. The two "L" section side timbers were put on first, followed by the three cross members. The central support was fitted next and when the adhesive had thoroughly set on these assembled pieces, the three angular struts each side were cut and put in place, (**Fig.2.21**).

Before anything else was done, the hawse holes were drilled. In retrospect, it would have probably been even better

to have drilled them before assembling the head timbers. One sudden cough or sneeze during the drilling operation can easily undo quite a bit of delicate work!

The kit provides 3mm square beech strip from which the rails are made. The secret here is to thoroughly steam the strip before attempting to apply pressure to attain the right degree of bending. I still favour the standard electric jug kettle for this task. The kettle was filled almost full with water and the strip dropped through the spout while the water was brought to the boil. I made a cardboard pattern for each of the rails and found

**Fig 2.24 The mast assemblies. Note the dowels at butt end.**

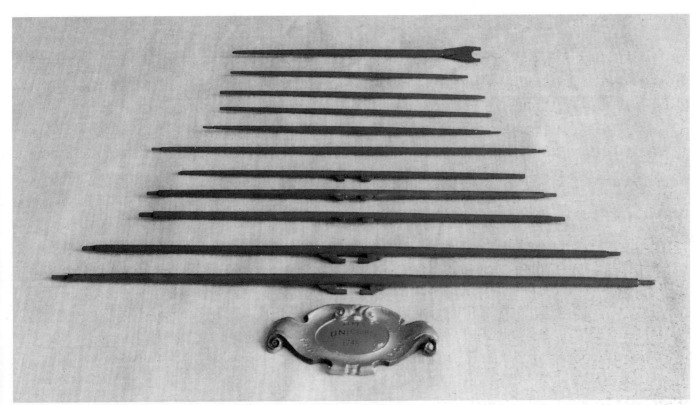

Fig 2.25 The yards and spars with sling and stop cleats where pertinent.

Fig 2.27 Stern view.

**Fig 2.27  Stern view.**

Fig 2.28 The figurehead and head timbers.

**Fig 2.29 The deck aft.**

that the wood could be bent easily with the fingers to conform to the pattern. Having made one, the opposite side was immediately made to match. The rails were bent and assembled to the hull and prow starting at the bottom. Having got the lowest pair in place, the two holes for the bowsprit gammoning were drilled and filed to shape. The top of the holes is coincident with the bottom edge of the lower rail and were introduced at this stage to avoid possible damage to the somewhat fragile assembly of the upper rails later on.

The addition of the figurehead completed the front end, (**Fig.2.22**). This was stuck in place using a two-part epoxy adhesive, with the casting held in place with an elastic band anchored around the catheads, (no pun intended). Incidently, don't leave the figurehead all shiny as supplied; it makes the model look as if it has come from a toy shop. Paint it with either an acrylic or Humbrol No.54 gold to give it a more antique-like appearance.

## The Bowsprit

You can have some fun and games with this feature if you don't keep your wits about you. The drawings are very clear with regard to the dimensions of the main components, but the fitting of the assembled unit to the hull is not depicted at all. In fact, from the dimensions you have to conclude that it is fixed to the front face of the forecastle - not an ideal fixing due to the small area involved. Drilling a hole 8mm dia. at the required angle at this stage would have been potentially very hazardous bearing in mind all the work just put in to make and assemble the head-rails.

I chose to make a technical adjustment, (in layman's terms, I cheated). First I drilled a 2mm dia. hole and dowelled the bowsprit in place. The cheating bit was putting a small flat on the underside of the bowsprit so that it sat tightly into the corner between the front face of the forecastle and the beakhead deck.

I also took into question the position of the fairlead saddle, that device with a series of holes in it that sits on top of the butt end of the bowsprit. The main assembly drawing shows it between the two sets of gammoning, whereas on a smaller detail drawing it is shown aft of the gammoning. However, my research led me to understand that it should have been forward of the gammon lashings and that is where I put it on my model.

The completed hull is shown in **Fig.2.23**.

## The Masts and Yards

The drawings provided a complete set of dimensions for pieces that go to make up the mast assemblies. One thing that I found worthwhile checking was the size of the square holes provided in the mast caps. They were a little smaller than the sections shown for the top ends of the relevant masts. Owing to the way in which the grain runs through the caps, I found that it was better to reduce the square section at the top of the masts just to the thickness of the caps. Apart from that, the mast assemblies were quite straightforward, (**Fig.2.24**).

For some reason Corel had not thought it necessary to consider holes in the gun deck to house the butt end on the masts, although the given dimensions for the length of the masts sug-

**Fig 2.30 Amidships.**

gest that such a fixing was intended. The main drawing and the section of the hull indicate that the bottoms of the masts sit on top of the gun-deck. At this stage, drilling through the gun-deck may have proved a little dodgy so, I checked the relative length of each mast, adjusted as required from the bottom end and fitted a 3mm dia. dowel.

Having done this, I took a forward look at the rigging requirements and fitted as many blocks as possible before stepping the masts, in spite of the fact that they are sequentially numbered far ahead of the stage so far reached. With only seven or eight different styles of block, I am surprised that Corel didn't allocate just seven or eight numbers and use them throughout. To fit them in the sequence recommended does not appear to have any distinct advantage, in fact, I would suggest to the contrary. I found too, that it was necessary to look at all of the rigging drawings to make sure which blocks had a loop on its underside. There were discrepancies between the sheets in this respect.

The yards were similarly well-dimensioned on the drawings but Corel have not shown sling cleats or stop cleats. As I wished to correct this omission, I made and fitted them before painting the spars, (**Fig.2.25**). Again, all blocks were identified and tied in place at this juncture.

## Rigging in General

One of the first tasks was to dye some of the thread black for use as standing rigging. Alternatively, the thread provided, all tan-coloured, can be replaced as required or the vessel rigged entirely in tan. I always like to recognise that the standing rigging was tarred up, but this is a personal choice; there are many museum models that don't subscribe to this procedure.

The masts were then stepped, making sure that everything was square and in correct alignment. Any slight adjustment needed was easily met by trimming the relevant side of the 3mm dia. dowel mentioned earlier for locating the bottom end of the mast into the gun-deck.

Although I had put as many of the rigging blocks as possible into place before stepping the masts, I followed the recommended sequence for the rigging proper.

As found so successful in the past for discouraging the adherence of dust to the rigging, I "fingered in" white PVA adhesive into each length of thread before actually tying it on. All lashings and knots were sealed with the merest spot of cyanoacrylate applied with a cocktail stick. Not only does this have an almost instant effect, it also permits a very close trimming of the loose ends. I have found over the years that a pair of manicurist's cuticle clippers are absolutely ideal for this task, being eminently more controllable than a scalpel.

A further aid to rigging is to use a smear of cyanoacrylate to stiffen the end of every line that has to be threaded through a block. This provides a very helpful built-in bodkin and certainly makes life a lot easier.

## The Standing Rigging

The gammoning is the first task to tackle. This was normally lashed such that it appeared to have a twist between stem and

**Fig 2.31 The fore deck.**

bowsprit. This was achieved by routing it to start from a forward position on the bowsprit to an aft position in the slot through the stem. After about ten turns the gammoning was frapped in the middle.

The shrouds and ratlines to all three masts were then rigged. This application was entirely conventional. The ratlines, as always, were a bit of a pain, although by virtue of repetition rather than difficulty. A sheet of stiff paper sprung between the channels and the underside of the relevant top helped to keep the eyes in focus. A series of parallel horizontal lines drawn at the correct separation also helped to keep the spacing reasonably even.

The fore, main and mizen stays, together with backstays from the upper masts to the channels completed the standing rigging, (**Fig.2.26**). However, I would warn that there are several misprints on the drawings with regard to the numbers allocated to belaying points. This was not a major problem to get round, since the instructions and the belaying diagram invariably gave the correct reference.

## The Running Rigging

The sequence of application shown in the instructions was followed and no difficulty was found in setting up this part of the rigging. The only deviation that I made from the instruction manual was to add the foot-ropes to the yards before setting the yards up on the masts. I found this to be much simpler than trying to do them afterwards.

One adverse comment that I would make, is the fact that the drawings and the box art show the yards set in a position where sails would be rigged. Without sails, the yards would normally be down almost on the caps. This is the way I have made my model. Apart from that there is not much else to say.

The sketches showing the way in which the various lines pass through the relevant blocks, and on down to their respective belaying points, were extremely clear and descriptive.

## Finishing Off

It only remained to rig the anchors and add all the coils of rope at the many belaying points around the vessel. It is essential to make sure that the coils are made up using the same size thread as used on that particular part of the rigging.

The nameplate provided in the kit needed to be painted and, for the inscription, I chose to use rub-down lettering. A bit of a fiddly job but, even so, better than I could have done freehand. The result can be seen again in **Fig.2.25**.

The flag, as is often the case with kits, was not correct. For the period, the correct flag to be flown at the stern would be the red British Naval Ensign without the red diagonal cross of St. Patrick, and not the white ensign provided in the kit. So, you have a choice; leave it off altogether or fly the correct one. Unfortunately, even if the right one comes to hand, it is not always easy to get it to hang right. Nothing looks worse than a stiff piece of material that looks as if it has had a good coat of starch and, in spite of the several adverse comments that I have made, this is a model that deserves better than that. See **Figs 2.27 to 2.31** for the finished model.

## Conclusions

This has been a rather difficult kit to assess in a fair and proper manner and you should not expect to build an accurate model of the vessel in question straight from the box. The historical notes were generally incorrect and, certainly, the date quoted was some 42 years adrift. However, having said that, the construction of the hull provided a reasonable presentation of the 1748 frigate and, in the case of the one or two deviating features, matters were easily put to rights without purchasing any additional parts or materials.

The rigging is an area that is open to discussion. My own gut feelings leave me very suspicious but, with definitive information not being available, I have gone along with what is portrayed in the kit. It certainly doesn't play the game according to Lees and his work on masting and rigging.

At the end of the day, you do get a very nice looking model and, subject to your own thoughts on the rigging, a fairly accurate one. Quite a lot of hours' work, even for the experienced modeller and, in the price bracket of £140-£150, a very reasonable buy.

## References

"The First Frigates" by Robert Gardiner. Conway Maritime Press ISBN 0 85177 601 9

"Eighteenth Century Rigs and Rigging" by Karl Heinz Marquardt. Conway Maritime Press ISBN 0 85177 586 1

"The Masting and Rigging of English Ships of War 1625-1860" by James Lees. Conway Maritime Press ISBN 0 85177 290 0

# CHAPTER 3

# THE ENGLISH BRIG *PORTSMOUTH*

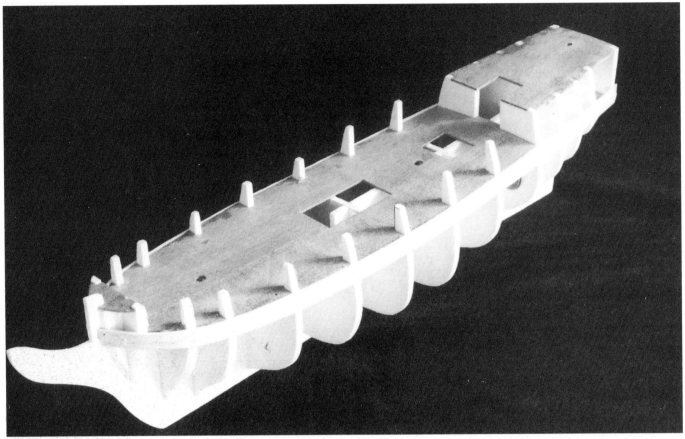

**Fig. 3.1 The basic hull carcase with false decks and first planks in place.**

Mamoli's kit is described as being for an English brigantine of 1796, armed with twelve carriage guns on the main deck. The two-masted, gaff rig is set up for royals and for studding sails at the topmast and topgallant levels. It provides for a neat little model and quite colourful should you choose to paint it as shown on the box art.

At 1/64 scale the finished model is 695mm long and 550mm high.

## The Kit

The drawings and instructions follow the established Mamoli procedures, being multilingual and fairly easily understood. All parts and operations are sequentially numbered and the parts lists give full dimensional details and are coded for material type. This involves reference back and forth to the code list, but really isn't too much hassle. The rigging and belaying is well-presented via a system which defines starting and finishing points with intermediate blocks and other tackle.

The materials are quite reasonable with accurate pre-cutting where applicable. The strip wood I found to be a little coarse-grained but straight and true in section.

The fittings tray contained castings for the figurehead, transom and quarter galleries. The blocks for rigging were extremely well-produced, having good shape and well-drilled holes.

Gun barrels and carriages, belaying pins, anchors and a pre-formed ship's boat provided a fairly comprehensive set of parts.

The white-edged ensign and jack are the right design for non- naval vessels after 1801 so, make the model to be six years in service and you'll be OK.

## Tools and Consumables

The usual craft knife, scalpel and razor saw are the main cutting tools required. Flat and half-round files or Perma-Grit tools will fulfil the abrasive needs, backed up by various grades of abrasive paper. A small electric drill will be most useful with a selection of twist drills up to about 2mm dia., together with a light hammer or pin pusher.

Looking at the planking material, you most certainly will split it if you don't drill holes to take the fixing pins. The instructions recommend soaking the planking strips prior to bending, but I found that this could mostly be avoided by using a plank nipper.

White PVA, contact adhesive such as Thixofix, and a bottle of cyanoacrylate should cover the sticking department.

There is quite a bit of painting to do, so surface preparation in the form of sanding sealer will prove advantageous. As for paint, I tend to use Humbrol acrylics. When stirred properly, they cover well and don't get absorbed by the wood, as is the case of some other paint designed, perhaps, more for plastic surfaces. The other big advantage, of course, is that your brushes can be cleaned with water and maybe a touch of washing-up liquid.

## Basic Hull Construction

The conventional bulkhead on false keel assembly provided a strong basis for the planking. Squareness and good alignment throughout was important but not difficult to achieve. Some adjustment to slot depths was necessary when making sure that the tops of the bulkheads were coincident with the deck

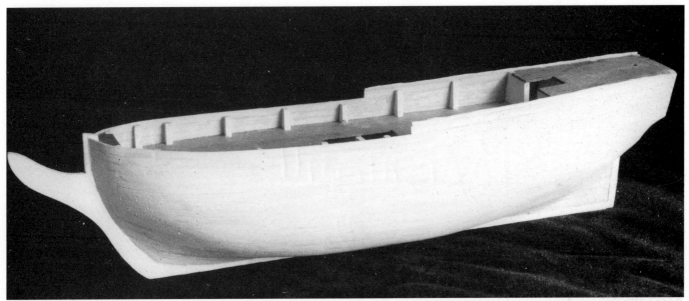

Fig. 3.2 **The first planking complete and rubbed down. Note that the planks above deck level are not glued to frame extensions.**

Fig. 3.3 **First painting coat can be conveniently applied as second planking progresses.**

levels of the false keel. Pre-shaped stern and bow blocks were glued in position and the assembly left for the adhesive to thoroughly cure. I found that the deck pieces, dry assembled, were ideal for keeping everything in place during this period.

The three deck parts were then glued and pinned in place to hold the camber. When the glue had set, I removed the pins and then started on the task of filing the edges of the bulkhead frames, bow and stern blocks, to match the curves of the hull. A planking strip was constantly in use to check that the subsequent sheathing would sit correctly.

The first planking was very straightforward. Starting at deck level and working down to the keel, (**Fig.3. 1**), the planks only needed tapering to about half width from amidships towards the stem. A plank nipper was perfectly adequate to bend the strip over the tapered length and each plank was glued to its neighbour and glued and pinned to each frame. The holes in the planks were drilled to avoid splitting. The few planks above deck level were added, taking care to glue them to each other, but not to the frame extensions which have to be removed later.

The pins were removed and the planking rubbed down smooth, (**Fig.3.2**). The second planking came in a variety of timbers, which provided contrast between the various levels above and below the wales should you choose not to paint the hull as specified on the drawings. Take care though, there is only just enough of each sort and none for spares should you make an error.

If you decide to paint the hull, it was found to be of considerable help to paint a first coat on each section of planking and the main wale as they were assembled, (**Fig.3.3**). Similarly, after the bulwarks had been lined and the gun-ports cut, those areas were also painted.

The bulwark rails are best made in several pieces. It is not really possible to bend the timber across the width of the section satisfactorily. The instructions make this recommendation for the pieces around the front end, but I found it easier to follow this procedure even for the more gentle curves towards the stern. The lined and painted bulwarks with fitted rails are shown in **Fig.3.4**.

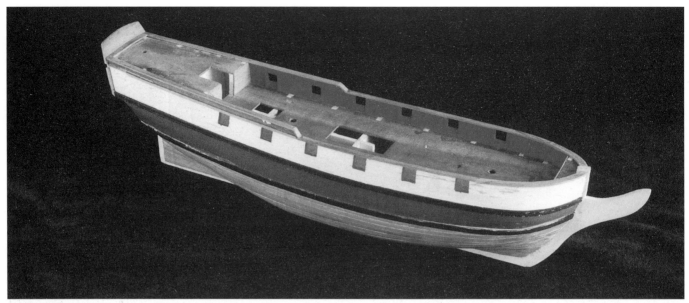

**Fig. 3.4 The frame extensions removed, inside bulwarks painted and rails fitted all round.**

**Fig. 3.5 Decks planked and gratings fitted.**

The poop and fore deck facings were added, followed by the construction of the door frame in the front of the poop deck. I found that it was a help to build this structure around the actual size of the cast door unit provided in the kit, albeit that in the end, I made my own pair of doors from odd scraps of strip which, to me, seemed to match better with the surrounding woodwork.

The deck planking was laid in 80mm lengths having positioned one entire strip centrally as a basic guide. I took par-

ticular care not to waste any of the strip material provided for this feature, since it was fairly obvious that there wasn't overmuch supplied. Gratings, deck planking and poop deck facing and doors are shown in **Fig.3.5**.

The rudder was then made up and hung to complete the basic hull assembly. The final coats of paint were added but the decks left unvarnished until the deck fittings had been put in place.

Making the stand at this juncture was found to be helpful in the ongoing fitting-out process.

Fig. 3.6 The finished hull from off the starboard bow.

Fig. 3.7 The completed hull from off the port quarter.

**Fig. 3.8** Assembled masts with advanced attachment of rigging blocks.

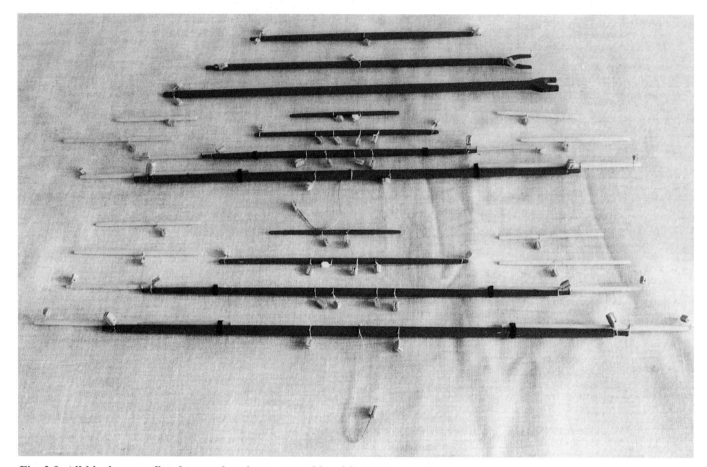

**Fig. 3.9** All blocks were fitted to yards prior to assembly with masts.

## Fitting Out

There were a number of deck fittings, many of which had to be fabricated from the timber provided. The boat shell and ship's wheel with mounting were ready formed. However, with regard to the boat, this obviously comes from a standard fittings list and the bottom is slotted to take the keel/stem post. The latter is normally part of the set up, but in this case it was missing, either by design or accident and had to be made from scrap.

The head-rails were largely made by assembling the various strips of material on the drawing. Some steaming and soaking was required to attain the curves involved, but it was really a matter of patience rather than difficulty.

The bitts and fife rails take quite a bit of load when the rig-ging is applied, so I considered it a good idea to dowel them to the deck with a short length of 1mm dia. wire. The pin rails, fitted to the inside of the bulwarks should also be well-secured for the same reason.

The cap that sits on the peak deck over the bowsprit need-ed some attention to angle the bore. A round file, gently applied, did the job quite well with constant checking for fit using a length of 6mm dia. dowel.

Channels and chain plates caused some moments of thought. The chain plates provided in the kit are longer than those depicted on the main drawing and totally different in design to those shown on the box art. It is largely a matter of adjusting the position of the channels on the hull sides and/or the fixing points at the lower end of the chain plates.

The completed fitting out is shown in **Figs. 3.6 & 3.7**.

**Fig. 3.10 The shrouds, ratlines and backstays to the foremast.**

## The Masts and Spars

The dowel rod provided was sorted into the various sizes required. It is always a good idea to check whether the various mast parts and spars can be randomly cut from the dowel rods. In many cases, it is found that only a certain combination of pieces can be cut from any particular length, without having pieces over; each too short to complete the set!

All tapering was done by first planing to octagonal section, then filing and finally spinning using abrasive paper. Square sections were filed on the top end of the masts after spinning. When assembling the various mast parts, the alignment of lower masts, topmasts and topgallants was constantly checked. It is important not to get it wrong in the hope that any discrepancy can be pulled out with the rigging.

There was some confliction in the painting instructions, in that the drawings and box art showed the masts to be white, whereas the instructions advised that they should be left natural wood. Take your choice. The yards were painted dark brown before assembling the stuns'l boom and irons.

The drawings clearly indicated where various blocks had to be attached to both masts and yards. However, the blocks are sequentially numbered with the rigging to which they are relevant but I have always found that the tying on of blocks is a task better done before stepping the masts into the hull. This is a personal choice and, for convenience, I marked the parts list to indicate those blocks that I chose to attach in advance of the rigging proper. Other model makers with younger and

less gnarled fingers may well find the sequential system OK. You do have to be careful and not lose any of the blocks and deadeyes; there were only just enough to complete the model.

The assembled masts and yards are shown in **Figs. 3.8 & 3.9** respectively.

## The Rigging

The standing rigging was the first to be set up. The drawings were extremely good, indicating sequence and position and the Mamoli system is as good as any you will find in a kit, particularly if you happen to be a relative beginner to the hobby.

You may wish, as I did, to use black thread for this part of the rigging. This involves, either replacing the tan thread provided or, resorting to dyeing. If you are happy with the tan thread then obviously you can ignore my last comment. Before each length of rigging was attached, it was pulled through white PVA gluey fingers to stiffen it and to lay down all the dust-catching surface fibres. The leading 10mm end of each line was then smeared with cyanoacrylate to produce a built-in "bodkin" for easier threading through blocks, etc. Various aspects of the standing rigging are shown in **Figs. 3.10, 3.11 & 3.12**.

Having completed the first stage of the rigging, the yards were then added to the masts in preparation for the running rigging. Again, the drawings are first class and there were no problems in seeing where everything had to go.

Fig. 3.11 The standing rigging to the main mast.

Fig. 3.12  The completed standing rigging.

Fig. 3.13  The fore top and upper shrouds.

**Fig. 3.14 Stern view.**

**Fig. 3.15 The bows and head rails.**

The kit included material for furled sails but after a couple of attempts to get a reasonable looking result I decided to leave them off altogether.

Anchors, flags and coils of rope, hung at the various pin-rails, put the final touches to the model. See **Fig.3.13 to 3.18** for finished model.

## Conclusions

I found this kit to be very good for the relative beginner. It had enough challenging constructional features to maintain interest and extremely good rigging instructions to guide the modeller through what sometimes appears to the uninitiated to be an absolute maze.

The drawings are well-detailed and the supporting parts lists give clear indication to the size and type of material for each item. Follow the recommended sequence through and you really can't go far wrong.

My main criticism was that there was only just enough of everything required. This undoubtedly is very cost effective, but it gives no latitude for errors and is very frustrating to the beginner who hasn't yet accumulated a spares box.

On the whole quite a nice package with ten out of ten for the rigging instructions. RRP £109.99.

Distributed by AMERANG Ltd. Commerce Way, Lancing, West Sussex.

**Fig. 3.16 Looking down on the main deck.**

**Fig. 3.17 The foredeck and windlass assembly.**

Fig. 3.18 The completed model.

# CHAPTER 4

# The See Ewer *Elbe*

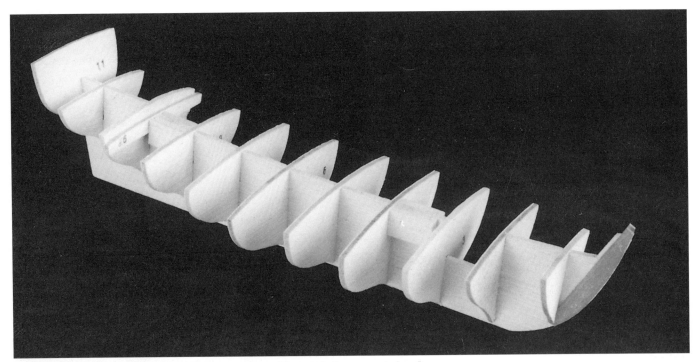

**Fig. 4.1 The hull carcase with mast supports and bow reinforcements in place.**

This kit from Constructo is for a See Ewer built about 1900. The basic design had been around since the Middle Ages and was for a wooden boat of shallow draft, with lee boards, making it most suitable for coastal work. This particular vessel was typical of hundreds used around the shores of the Baltic Sea.

## The Kit

Constructo have produced a well-presented kit with good quality materials and fittings. The compartmentalised system of packing is enhanced by bagged items, each bag also con-taining outline drawings and identification of the bits con-cerned. A nice touch, this, which will help any newcomer to the hobby get a feel for how everything comes together. The frames are pre-cut and the deck parts are easily pressed out of the ply sheets supplied. The one sheet drawing provides the details required to build a model some 21.5in (545mm) long at a scale of 1/52. The multilingual instruction manual is ade-quate and a novice modeller should not have too much trouble achieving an acceptable result, provided that some care and thought are put into the project. Although originally conceived as a single-planked hull, the kit does now contain material for a second, thinner planking.

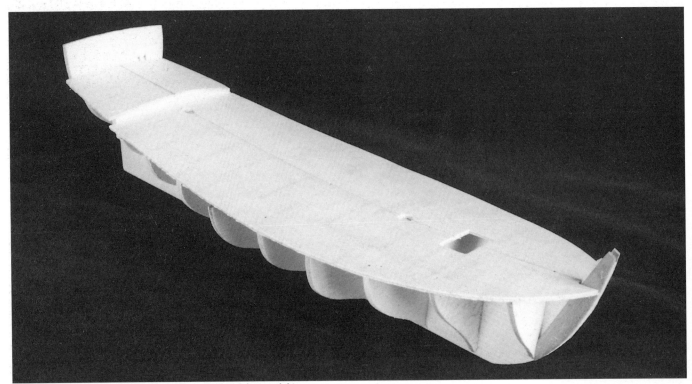

**Fig. 4.2 The false decks pinned and glued in position.**

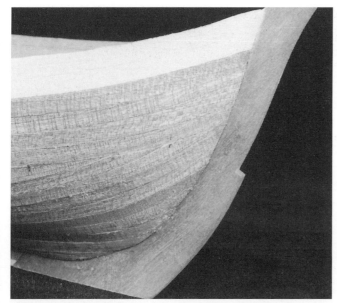

Fig. 4.3  The second planking ready for rubbing down. The planks fit snugly against the stem.

## Tools

Although not particularly difficult to build, this model does require something more than a craft knife and glue. A razor saw and David plane, together with a miniature electric drill are fairly essential items. Due mainly to the thickness of the first planking material, some means of bending the planks will be required over and above a plank nipper. The instruction manual makes several suggestions in this regard. The usual selection of various grades of abrasive paper for the inevitable rubbing down should be to hand, together with some white PVA adhesive and some cyanoacrylate.

## Making the Hull

The ply frames were slotted into the false keel and mast support blocks added, (**Fig.4.1**). Although this is a fairly small craft, you have to watch the relative frame alignment in order to get everything square and true. A little bit of packing in the cross-halving joints, where appropriate, helped to wedge any wayward frame in place while the glue set. Further reinforcements at the prow were glued in place in order to increase the keel thickness, thus providing something on to which the hull planking could be pinned.

The false decks were then glued and pinned in place, (**Fig.4.2**), and the edges of the deck and frames shaped to the longitudinal lines of the hull ready for planking. The deck planking pieces were cut and assembled using one continuous central plank as a guide. The outer planks were allowed to overlap the edges of the false deck, then trimmed off after the glue had thoroughly dried. It was important to sand the deck surface to the final finish required at this stage since this operation would be extremely difficult after assembling the bulwarks.

The hull planking, it has to be said, was a bit of a pig. This was nothing to do with the lines of the hull which are relatively simple, but concerned the 2mm thickness of the planking strips. Bearing in mind that Constructo now provide a second, thinner, set of planking strips, the basic set could really be reduced to at least 1.5mm or, even better, 1mm thickness. However, 2mm is what was there and it needed a lot of soaking, heat and gentle coercion to get into shape. My favourite plank nipper was definitely not man enough for the job, so the electric kettle was used to boil up and soak the forward ends of the planks.

One edge of the planks needed shaping to allow them to lie

Fig. 4.4  The finished planked hull with overlength keel for later matching with rudder width.

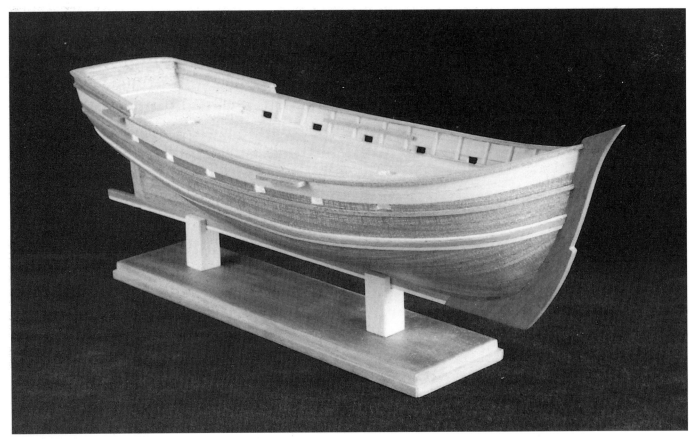

**Fig. 4.5 The assembled rails and stanchions.**

snugly against one another without a large gap. All planks were both glued with white PVA and pinned to the frames and to each other. The planks above the deck line that formed the bulwarks could only be glued edgewise to each other. These were fitted one at a time and held in place with small crocodile clips until the glue had set.

When all planks had been fitted, the whole surface was rubbed down, filled and given a coat of sanding sealer ready for the second planking.

Before doing the thinner, second sheathing, the stem and

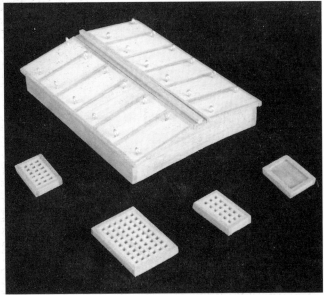

**Fig. 4.6 The various gratings and hatches ready for assembly.**

keel were assembled. It is very difficult to produce a width of surface around the bows to exactly match the thickness of the stem post and conform to shape, thus, by fitting them before applying the second planking, the ends of the planks can be neatly snugged in against the side of the stem to provide a much neater result. The keel was left a little overlength so that it could be matched correctly to the rudder width later on.

The thinner, second sheathing was relatively straightforward to apply. A contact adhesive was used to avoid the warping that would have occurred if the less viscous PVA had been employed. Each plank was carefully angled at the bow end to fit snugly against the stem post, (**Fig.4.3**), and allowed to overlap the stern by about 3mm for later trimming. A plank nipper was used to produce the curves required fore and aft. The complete hull at this stage is shown in **Fig.4.4**.

The waterways, transom facings, stanchions and bulwark rails were then added, (**Fig.4.5**). The rails are made up of three strips, applied separately but laminated together to form a 5mm width. This was an excellent way to get around the obvious difficulties involved in bending a single 5mm strip across its width.

The wales and rubbing strakes also comprised small section strips and were fixed in a fairly simple but effective manner. The side of the hull was marked to indicate the line of the wale or strake and, the bow end of the strip was cut to fit tight up against the stem. A touch of cyanoacrylate applied to about the first 30mm length of the strip permitted it to be firmly fixed in place. Another drop of the same adhesive was then put on to the blade of a craft knife which was then used to stroke along the contact surface of the strip for about 75mm. Following the marks on the hull, the strip was laid in place.

**Fig. 4.7 Internal view of the cabin showing scrap 3mm square corner fillet.**

This operation was repeated over the full length of the hull. The advantages of this method are that there are no holding devices necessary and that the fixing is more or less immediate. This completed the basic hull structure, again see **Fig.4.5**.

## The Stand

Unlike many other kits, Constructo have provided materials to make a stand and, this was the time to make it up, to provide a support for the hull during the following stages of construction. It was very simple to put together and all that was needed to give a nice finish was a good rub down and a couple of coats of gloss varnish. The finished article is just right for the job, nothing too ornate to take the eye from the finished model.

## Fitting Out

There was nothing too difficult in making up the various items that had to be fitted to the deck. Each one was treated as a mini-project and, with some of the parts prefabricated, work progressed quite readily. However, there were one or two procedures that might help the absolute beginner to produce a more satisfying job.

It was seen that the loading hatch was made up of two and three pieces of 5mm x 2mm strip glued edge to edge. These were cut overlength and glued together first so that all final cutting and assembly was done with 10 x 2mm. Similarly the covers comprised 13 x 2mm edged on both sides with 2 x

**Fig. 4.8 Exterior view of cabin before rubbing down.**

**Fig. 4.9 The cabin without roof.**

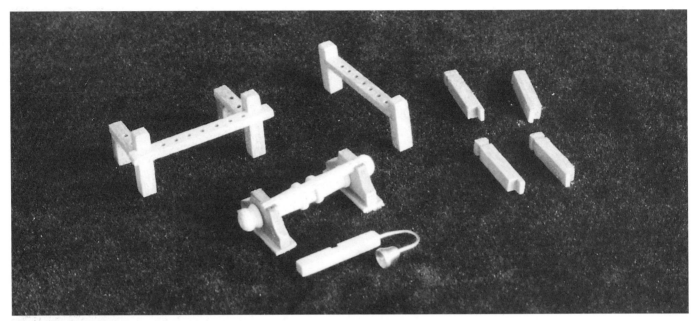

Fig. 4.10  the windlass, bitts and pin racks.

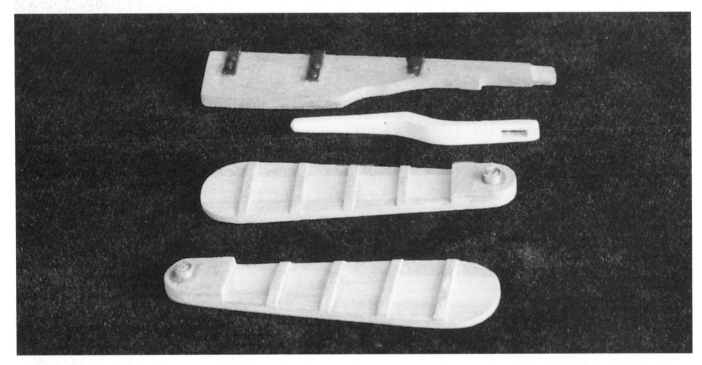

Fig. 4.11  Leeboards, tiller and rudder.

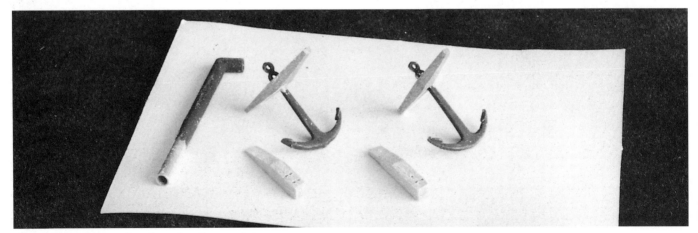

Fig. 4.12 Anchor, catheads and galley stack.

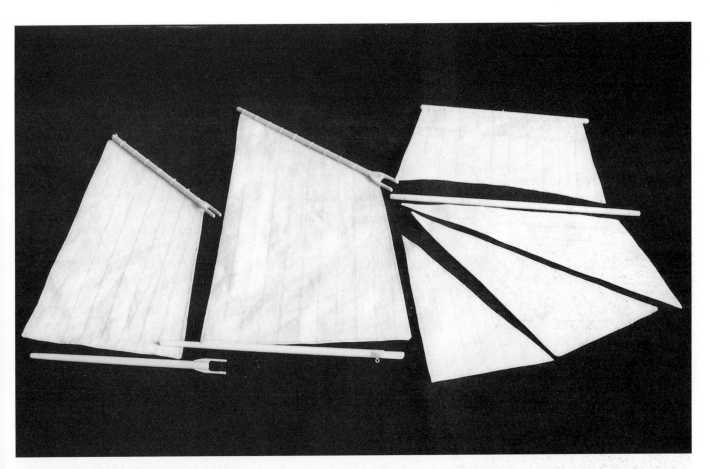

Fig. 4.13 The sails with booms and gaffs.

Fig. 4.14 The forward part of the completed hull.

1mm. Again, a strip 360mm long of the former size was edged before cutting the twelve individual covers each 28mm long. Six of these pieces were then glued together in a line against a straight edge and the adhesive allowed to thoroughly dry. The actual overall length of this sub-assembly was then used as a basis for making up the hatch sides and ends. The completed loading hatch and gratings are shown in **Fig.4.6**.

The cabin was a more involved project than the brief instruction leads you to believe. The sides of the cabin are made up by gluing planking strips edge to edge. The strips immediately adjacent to the windows should be edged with a lighter strip first before cutting to length and assembling. Unfortunately, the instructions dodge the tricky bit - putting the four sides together. I got around the difficulty by gluing a piece of 3mm square scrap to the upright edges of each side then, when dry, shaped the front and rear faces to the angle required to make a snug fitting corner fillet, (**Fig.4.7**). Cyanoacrylate was then used to bring all four sides of the cabin together, ensuring that the front and rear pieces did not overlap the sides. Strips of 2mm square were let into the outside corner recesses and sanded flush, (**Fig.4.8**). The assembled four sides are shown in **Fig.4.9**. The roof was then added, planked and trimmed.

The pin racks, winch and hatches were relatively simple to make and fit, (**Fig.4.10**). A check was made on the number and disposition of all the deck-mounted eyebolts and these too were fixed at this stage. It was found that a hole drilled 0.7mm dia. was just right to accept the shank of the eyebolt material. These were all fitted using fine-nosed pliers and a touch of cyanoacrylate. The leeboards, tiller and rudder are shown in **Fig.4.11** and the anchors, catheads and galley stack in **Fig.4.12**.

## The Masts and Spars

Apart from a couple of the smaller diameter items, these all had to be tapered. I used a David plane and file to first shape the dowel rod to octagonal section, then spun them in my small lathe to sand down to the required round section. If you do not have a lathe available, all of these parts are small enough to safely spin in an electric drill with care. If you have a holder for the drill to keep it firm, so much the better. None of the tapers were found to be very severe and, in fact, if you are in any way adept with a file, spinning might not be absolutely necessary.

Before stepping the two masts, all the eyebolts were put in place and any holes through masts and spars were drilled. It was seen that the gaffs should not be assembled at this stage, but left to be lashed to the sails at a later juncture.

Views of the hull, ready for rigging, are shown in **Figs. 4.13 to 4.16**.

## Sails

The sail material was quite a nice quality, but rather too white. Before cutting out the individual sails, which are already marked out, I soaked the whole sheet of material in weak tea for a while to take away the brightness. The sheet was then

**Fig. 4.15 the complete hull aft.**

Fig. 4.16 The completed hull with masts stepped ready for rigging.

Fig. 4.17 The standing rigging set up.

pinned to my drawing board and all the seams and hem lines drawn in with a chisel-pointed-brown-coloured pencil. Before removing the sheet, it was given a good coat of acrylic matt varnish and left to dry. This gets round the need to hem the edges of the sails which, when cut actual size from the sheet, won't fray or have a stitched hem that is totally out of scale. The edges are also strong enough to withstand the passing of a fine needle for any rigging necessary without the holes pulling out.

The above procedure is one that I use mainly because I am pretty hopeless at sewing, both with needle and sewing machine. Obviously, for those model makers with the right talent, machining the hems and seams may be the more desirable option. The main problems at this scale are to get a small enough hem and to ensure that the seams are truly parallel.

## Rigging

The instructions, unfortunately, do not give much in the way of guidance as to the way to approach the rigging.

A couple of general notes. All thread was pulled through fingers smeared with PVA adhesive. This lays down all the hairy surface fibres and reduces the later picking up of dust particles. The threading end of each line was smeared with cyanoacrylate to stiffen the end. This provided a built-in bodkin for easier reeving of blocks etc.

The standing rigging was the first to be set up - the stays and shrouds. The latter were rigged to the chainplates via lanyards between deadeyes. It was important to recognise the correct attitude of the deadeyes, the holes being positioned as shown on the drawings. Imagining a triangle formed by the three holes, the apex of the triangle is at the top in the upper deadeye of each pair and at the bottom in the lower deadeye.

The stays were then set up, the fore stays to the bowsprit and the backstays from the main mast down to the deck via blocks and tackle, (**Fig.4.17**). Note that the tackle part of the set-up, because it runs through blocks, should be in tan-coloured thread rather than the darker colour that represents tarred rope.

There are two different types of block provided in the kit; single hole and double hole. The latter were supposed to be marked with a "X" on the drawings but, in fact, they were not all marked on all views so it was advisable to study the drawings at length in this respect to identify them. There are also one or two printing errors on the belaying diagram where pin numbers 66 -79 have been labelled 166-179. Nothing very disastrous, but a bit disconcerting to the newcomer.

Before starting the running rigging, the two gaff sails were lashed to their respective gaffs and the square topsail lashed to its yard, again see **Fig.4.13**. It also helped to tie all blocks in place before assembling the gaffs and yards to the masts.

It is often very easy to pull things out of kilter by overtightening the rigging. To avoid this, I usually do a dry run, grouping those

**Fig. 4.18 Barrels and bucket in place on the fore deck.**

**Fig. 4.19 The anchor rigging.**

**Fig. 4.20 The cabin and rear mast area.**

**Fig. 4.21  A view on the port quarter.**

Fig. 4.22  The spars on the fore mast.

Fig. 4.23  The deck aft.

Fig. 4.24  The forward deck and windlass.

**Fig. 4.25 The sweeping lines of the prow.**

**Fig. 4.26 The shrouds and lower deadeyes.**

**Fig 4.27 The rudder and tiller assembly.**

lines that are relevant to each other, and particularly those that are in pairs, port and starboard. The belaying end of each line is passed through its appropriate hole in the pin rack and held in place by dropping in the belaying pin. This permits later adjustment to get the system balanced after which the belaying can be made permanent.

## Finishing Off

Barrels and buckets were put in place according to the positions shown on the drawing, (**Fig.4.18**). The anchors were rigged, (**Fig.4.19**), and coils of thread made up to hang at the various belaying points, (**Fig.4.20**). This is an item missed in the instructions of many kits and is something that promotes a bit of realism. **See Fig.4.21 to 4.27** for finished model.

## Conclusions

The model maker should not be misled by the relatively small size of this model into thinking that this is a project that can be completed in a few hours. There is a considerable amount of detail and items like the cabin have to be dealt with in several stages. However, there is nothing terribly difficult if one exercises the normal amount of patience and care.

The model encompasses most of the procedures found in larger projects but, not too much rigging and not too many sails. In fact, the kit could almost be recommended as being an ideal kit for a relative beginner. I say, almost, because the possible problem for the novice will be the bending and fitting involved in the first planking. Without doubt, the kit would be much enhanced if the specification of material for this was changed to a more malleable and thinner section of wood, say 5 x 1.5mm lime. A little bit of drawing overhaul would also be required to bring the kit into the wider novice range.

However, having made those minor criticisms, the results are quite rewarding. The basic quality of materials and fittings is very good, permitting you to finish up with a very neat and trim model.

# CHAPTER 5

# THE SPANISH 17TH CENTURY 104-GUN SHIP *SAN FELIPE*

San Felipe 1690

The San Felipe is typical of the Spanish 104-gun war-ship built in the late 17th Century. It is ornate and colourful, full of character and detail, and certainly a worthwhile challenge to the model ship builder.

The model itself is pretty big, being 960mm overall length with a beam of 200mm and so, by the time you have the masts and yards on, you are going to need quite a large space to exhibit it.

## The Kit

If you can't park your car fairly near to the model shop, then take a friend with you or hire a fork-lift truck, you certainly won't want to carry the weight of this box very far! It really is a colos-

sus in every sense of the word, but then, I suppose it should be when you aren't going to get too much change from £600.

Seventeen ply sheets were all accurately laser cut, com-pletely eliminating any use of the fret-saw, (**Fig.5.1**). Strip wood came in lime, maple and walnut, all straight and clean, (**Fig.5.2**). The fittings packs, as you would expect, provided almost everything you can think of; gun barrels, blocks and deadeyes, gratings, anchors, capstan, stanchions, etc., (**Fig.5.3**). It was also very nice to find packs of decent pins with sharp points and well-formed heads. So often the points are malformed and the heads insufficient in size to aid extrac-tion from the planking.

The decorative castings were wrap-packed on identifying card sheets so that there was absolutely no doubt as to where

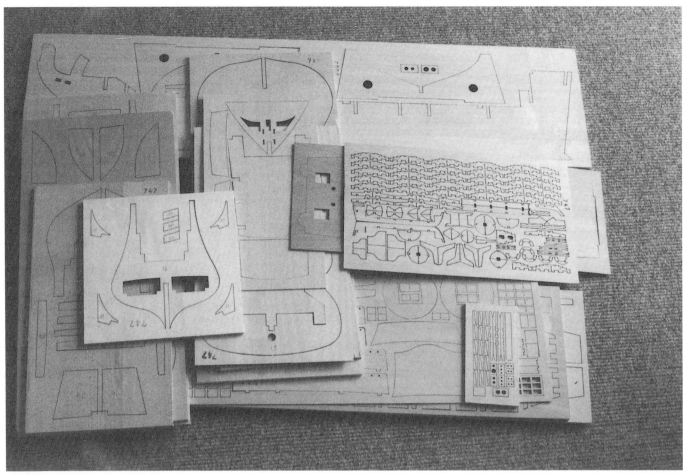

**Fig. 5.1 Laser cut ply panels.**

**Fig. 5.2 The strip material**

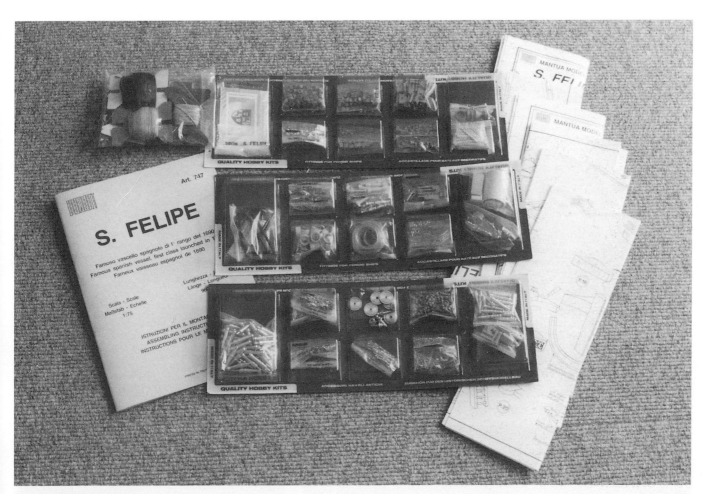

**Fig. 5.3 Fittings packs.**

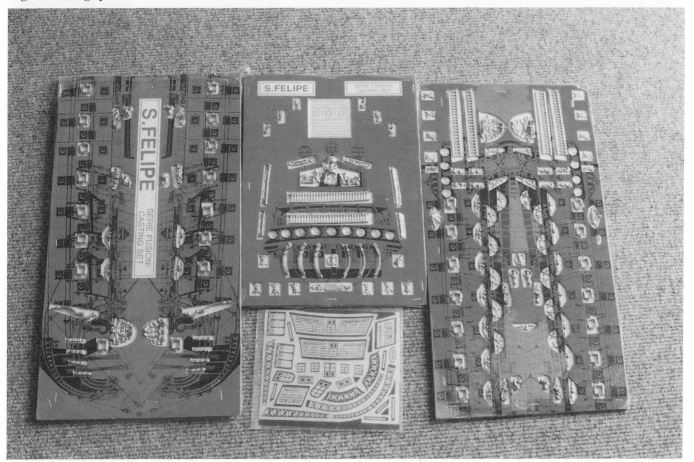

**Fig. 5.4 Castings and engraved sheet.**

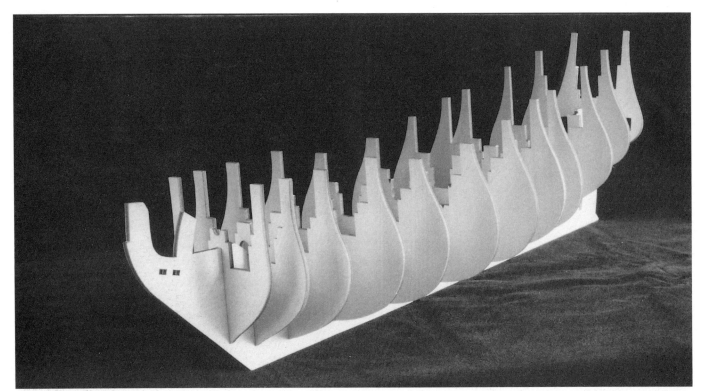

Fig. 5.5 The basic framework complete.

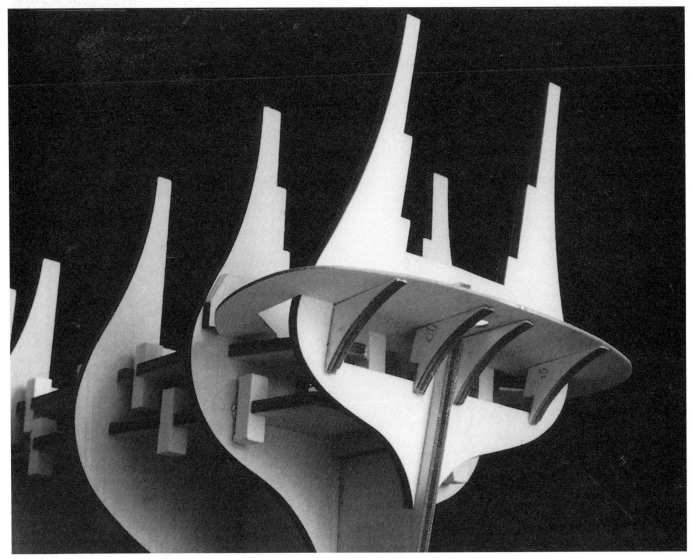

Fig. 5.6 The lower stern gallery.

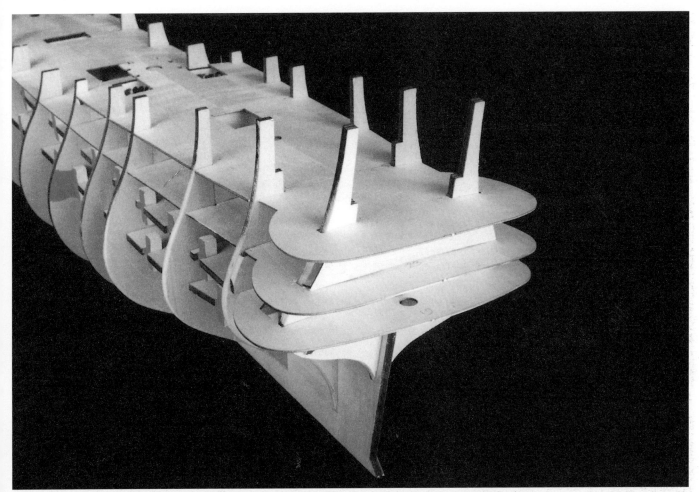

**Fig. 5.7  The false decks in place.  The faces of the gun barrel supports have been painted red.**

everything was intended to fit, (**Fig.5.4**). These were supported by a brass photo-engraved sheet and strips of moulded brass wire.

The construction was carefully and clearly illustrated on five double-sided sheets of drawings. The multilingual instruction manual provided a concise and sequential guide to the way in which everything went together. Some may think an instruction manual at this level of modelling was a little superfluous, particularly in view of the excellent construction details shown on the drawings. There were, however, several procedures in the hull construction where doing things in the right order was imperative. Thus, even the more experienced would do well to at least read the instructions, if only to identify these essential sequences.

## Tools

A 12 volt electric drill with capacity up to about 3mm diameter would be a great asset and, similarly, a small lathe for turning or sanding masts and spars. A selection of files, drills, tweezers and pliers will all prove to be very handy. The usual craft knife or scalpel with various shaped blades, abrasive papers of medium to fine grades and a few small crocodile clips or toolmaker's clamps should just about complete the necessary toolkit. White PVA adhesive for all the main woodwork, two-part epoxy for the metal bits and some cyano-acrylate for the quick and fiddly items will satisfy the sticky department.

A couple of, perhaps, more luxury items that made life much easier, were a set of Perma-Grit abrasive tools and a 12v Mini Craft disc sander.

You are going to need quite a bit of space to work in. The early work involves the hull carcase which is quite a handful and, as you progressively make or tittivate pieces to add to it, you want space to put the main framework to one side. Definitely not a project for the dining room table!

I would also suggest that, because of the large amount of sanding dust that is produced, two other items ought to be to hand. Regular use of a small vacuum cleaner to keep the work area clear and a face mask to avoid inhaling the dust.

## Forward Planning

It may seem a bit unnecessary, to say to people who are building a kit of this standard, to read the instructions before starting the construction of the model. However, with all the cast decoration to consider, it is worthwhile running through the build sequence and marking a few salient dimensions on the drawings. The lines of the wales and their relative positions with stern galleries and gun-ports are of particular importance, checking all the while that the spaces left for the placing of decorative pieces are large enough. You may also find, as I did, that there are several stages whose sequence could be altered to advantage. For instance, I found that the gun-port lids were more conveniently fitted and rigged at a later stage than that suggested in the instruction manual. These sort of decisions are not crucial to the building of the model, but merely reflect your own experience and way of working. This planning procedure is important and is worth spending quite a bit of time on and will certainly pay dividends in the long run.

## The Hull Carcase

The accuracy of the laser cutting in this kit was almost perfect. The slots in the frames, the stiffeners (16 and 17) and false keel, needed very little attention. It was deemed wise to make up a dry assembly using these parts before committing the glue pot. It was noted that the two banks of stiffeners sit horizontally within the carcase, so I first checked that the two related seating surfaces were the same distance apart on each of the frames. They were, but it is worth the check because, when assembled, they hold the whole framework true.

When assembling the frames to the false keel, a straight-edge was laid along the seating surfaces for the lower stiffener so that any adjustment to slot depths in the false keel could be made to bring everything into line. All frames except No.12 were then glued in place. Slotting the stiffeners on to the outside of the frames kept them square while the glue dried. The blocks for mounting the dummy gun barrels were cut and assembled to the stiffeners and, when dry, the latter were put into place within the frames, (**Fig.5.5**).

Another dry run, this time using the parts for the lower stern gallery, correctly identified the position of the last frame (No.12). These items were then glued in position, (**Fig.5.6**).

At this juncture, I decided to paint the outer surfaces of the gun mounting blocks which will be seen through the gun ports on the completed model. They don't have to be painted at this stage of course, or even at all, but if you wish to colour them, for best convenience the painting needs to be done before you start the planking.

The decks and their supports were all assembled in easy stages, again doing a dry run before permanently fixing. One stage in particular that I would draw attention to is the stern gallery support No.12b. Do not fix it in place on frame No.12 before slotting gallery No.23 in place. In this respect, Fig.11 on Drawing Sheet 1 is pictorially incorrect. Assembled decks are shown in **Fig.5.7**

The three transom support blocks were left overnight for the glue to thoroughly cure before attempting to shape their rear surfaces for seating the transom. The lower and smaller transom piece 31 was fixed in place first, and gave a good guide to the alignment of the larger transom plate 32. Both of these parts are curved and were clamped in place while the glue dried, (**Fig.8**).

The facings for the poop and quarter decks were then planked and the doors made up as indicated on the drawing. After gluing these in place, the edges of the frames were bevelled as required to provide a fair seating for the planking. I found that the first four frames at the bow and the last four at the stern, were the candidates for the heaviest chamfering. The carcase was now ready to start planking.

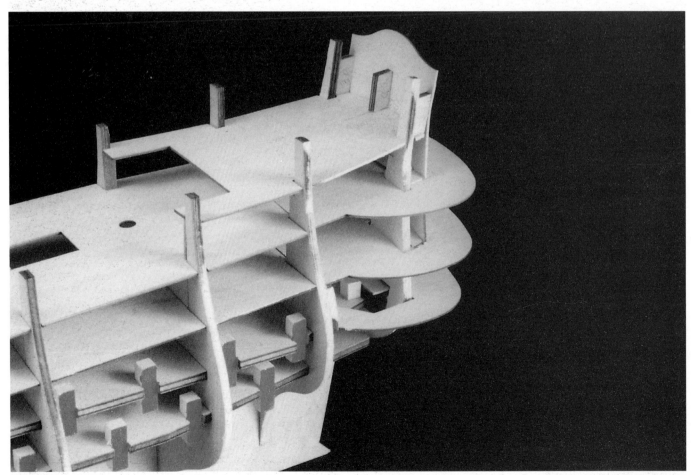

**Fig. 5.8 The upper and lower transom plates are curved. The three blocks supporting the upper plate were shaped after letting the glue thoroughly set.**

## The First Planking

The drawings and parts list show that the first planking should be in 7 x 1.5mm lime. Unfortunately, the material provided in the kit was only 6mm wide, thus the plank numbering on the drawing was redundant; nothing very serious, but obviously adjustments had to be made. In fact, the second planking, correctly supplied at 7mm width, can be applied without having any coincident longitudinal joints which adds to the total strength of the hull.

I managed all of the first planking using only a plank nipper for those planks that needed bending. It will be found that the planks sit on the frames better if you overbend rather than underbend. Planks were glued to each frame and edgewise to each other except, of course, above the various deck levels, where edge gluing only was the order of the day.

I started at the level of the quarter-deck, as suggested, and worked down to the level of the beak deck with untapered planking. I made a small spacing gauge from five short pieces of planking strip and divided the lower hull into separate sections six planks wide at the 'midships frame. Each section was then planked in, port and starboard alternately, until the first planking was complete, (**Fig.5.9**). All planks at the stern end were left with a short overlap in order to overlay the edges of the transom planking. Before commencing the second planking, the ends of the planks that come up to the stern post were thinned right down to about 0.5mm thickness and the whole outer surface sanded smooth.

This latter operation is always a very dusty procedure and this particular hull, because of its large size, was no exception. However, to keep the task as least time consuming as possible, I have come to favour the use of a Mini Craft Orbital Finishing Sander but fitted with a piece of Perma-Grit flexible strip. Just don't press too hard, or you will go right through the planking!

The "vertical" planking around the stern gallery needed some thought. The planks at the sides of the vessel lean inwards at the top, but there was a transitional change of angle, through the vertical, to a lean inwards towards the bottom around the stern. The vertical portion came at about 45° around the corner at each side. For that area 15° either side of the vertical position, i.e., from 30° to 60°, I used tapered pieces of planking, the taper being 6mm at the wide end to 2mm at the other. These were applied alternately, wide end and narrow end at the top to accommodate the the different angle of lean. The remainder was planked in with 6mm wide parallel strips.

## The Second Planking

I chose to use Thixofix contact adhesive for this part of the planking process. However, to attain total contact of the second planking on the first planking, the tapering, and the establishing of the position of key planks must be carefully done.

When I looked at the strips provided, it was obvious that

**Fig. 5.9  The first planking complete with the first strip of the second planking in place.**

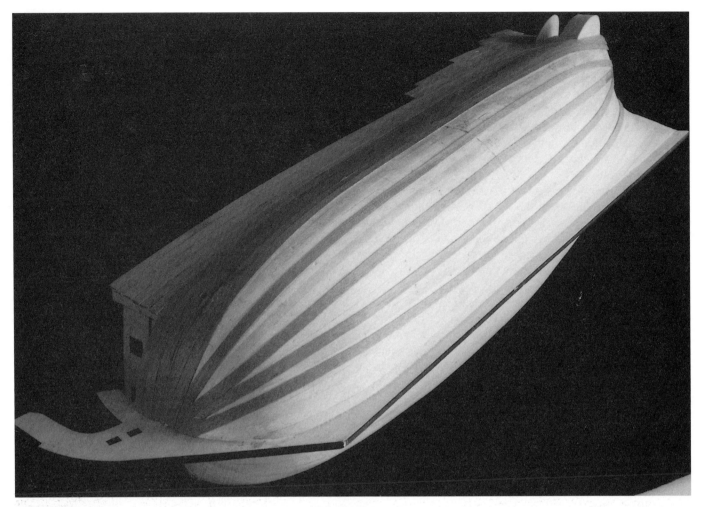

**Fig. 5.10 Master planks following the natural curves of the hull.**

there were two or three different shades of timber to consider. Now bearing in mind that the lower hull was ultimately to be painted, it was only necessary to select strips of the same shade for the area above the waterline. It may be, of course, that when all the gun-ports were cut and the decoration put on, different shades of timber wouldn't be obvious. However, I didn't take the chance.

The first plank was laid along the top of the forecastle bulwarks (again see **Fig.5.9**), followed by the remaining upper planks to the top of the poop deck. This gave some additional strength to all the bulwark planking while the lower hull was being worked on. Planks down to the level of the beak deck were all untapered.

Below that level, to use the full length planking strips supplied and as indicated on the drawings, you need to carefully position several key planks that naturally follow the curves of the hull, then fill in between them with strips tapered to suit, (**Fig.5.10**). I found that a spacing of three planks width, or 21mm, between the key planks worked out very well. If you try to follow one plank after the other down to the keel, you will find that they won't lay flat against the surface of the first planking and will thus present an horrendous job to sand to a smooth finish. When filling in between the key planks, I found that it was best to start at the upper side of the lower plank and work upwards towards the underside of the key plank above, shaping the ends of each successive plank as the filling-in process proceeded.

Inevitably, there were several stealers necessary at the stern end of the hull but, overall, the hull was reasonably straightforward to plank. The completed second planking is shown in **Fig.5.11**.

## Deck Planking

The instructions suggest that the strip material for the deck planking be cut into identical lengths of 8cm. To be honest, having used this method on a previous project, I was not particularly keen on this approach for such large areas. I chose instead to use full length strips and then, later, marked the butts with a pencil. This helped considerably in keeping the longitudinal alignment true.

My first task was to blacken one edge of each plank with a felt-tipped marker pen. One strip was then laid centrally along the centre line of each deck area to be planked and left to thoroughly set. This acted as the main alignment guide for each of the adjacent planks, (**Fig.5.12**). All off-cuts were kept for the planking of those smaller areas such as the stern galleries since there isn't overmuch material provided for this part of the project.

After all decks had been satisfactorily covered, they were sanded smooth and the butts marked in. The drawings showed butts on the same frames every other plank. This was certainly incorrect and I chose to use a three-shift-butt system, marking in the positions with a pencil. A useful tip for anyone choosing to adopt this method, is to use a draughtsman's propelling pencil that uses fine leads. It results in lines of all the same thickness without having to constantly sharpen the pencil.

## The Bulwark Rails

Slowly, slowly, catchee monkee, is the recipe for success here. Before applying any of the rails, a few dimensional and positional checks are advised. These were all designed to ensure that the height of the bulwarks was indeed high enough. The line of the gun-ports, the level of the beak deck and the position of the wales are all related. Since the line of the bulwarks was governed by a cardboard template which, in turn, controlled the position of the gun-port template, you will see that it was imperative that everything was hunky-dory before I got too committed with the rails.

A further check that was worthwhile was to consider the position of some of the brass decoration. Some pieces fitted between wales and the underside of the bulwark rails and I did not relish the thought of serious rectification at a later stage. The more experienced modeller would be well aware that in many kits, even at the luxury end of the market, the cast decorative items are not always exactly the same sizes as those shown on the drawings. So, as I have said, a bit of forward checking could be time well spent. Obviously any discrepancies found should be

rectified before any further work is done.

The inner faces of the bulwarks now had to be lined. Many of the gun-ports that have to be cut later come through into this lining and it is therefore imperative that, to help avoid break-out, the lining planks must be totally adhered to the core planking.

Having satisfied that condition, the application of the rails was then considered. The first problem was the slight bend against the width of the 6 x 2mm strip. Fortunately, those pieces with this feature were those where the rear portion could be glued firmly to the top of the hull side with a dowel into the 6 x 5mm block below, (**Fig.5.13**). When the glue had completely set, the front part of the rail was bent until its forward end could be dowelled into the relevant 6 x 5mm support. The ten end dowels, incorporating bollards, were turned on my small 12v Amati lathe to the dimensions shown on the drawings.

I started this part of the project at the lowest rail and gradually worked upwards, adding rails and blocks section by section, ensuring that glue had properly dried before moving on to the next level.

## The Beak and Forecastle Decks

The beak deck was planked and trimmed, then its slots adjusted for correct fit and seating. I chose to fit the gratings before

**Fig. 5.11 The second planking completed.**

**Fig 5.12 Deck planking under way. The central full length strip was used as a longitudinal guide.**

assembly, considering that it would be an easier task at this stage rather than leave them until later as indicated in the instructions.

The supports columns and beams for the forecastle deck were put in place, their positions being taken from the plan view of the completed vessel.

The front facing of the forecastle deck/beak deck was vertically planked, the two gun-ports cut and the hole for the bowsprit sized.

The forecastle deck itself posed a bit of a problem. There was a 20mm diameter hole in the pre-cut ply deck and, for the life of me I couldn't see what it was for. Reference to the drawings and instructions gave no clue that I could find and so, on the basis that I could do something about it later if necessary, I removed the 20mm diameter disc and planked over the hole. The deck was then fitted to the hull.

## Completing the Bulwark Rails

This involved drilling a series of 2mm dia. holes, regularly spaced, through both the upper and lower rails. These holes were drilled vertically and square with the waterline rather than perpendicular to the surface of the rails. Dowelling of 2mm dia. was then glued and inserted into each hole and cut off. When all holes had been filled, the protruding ends of the dowels were filed flush with the upper surface of the rail, (**Fig. 5.14**).

The only criticism I had of this part of the project con-

cerned the laser cut semi-circular rails for the top of the roundhouses at the fore end of the forecastle. 'Tis a pity they were not of the same wood to match the rest of the railing and needed a touch of paint to disguise the difference, (again see **Fig.5.14**).

## Positioning the Gun-Ports

A cardboard template is provided with all the positions marked and it is supposed to be as simple as pinning it to the side of the hull and transferring those points ready for drilling. However, before committing the drill, it was seen wise to make a few dimensional checks to be on the safe side. Another useful aid was to make up one of each of the two types of carriage gun, so that the height to the centre of the barrels from the deck surface could be compared with the template positions. On my model, I found that the template positions for these guns needed to be raised slightly so that the barrels poked through the ports centrally. The positions for the two lower rows of dummy barrels were found to be just right. I centre-popped all positions and then eyeballed down the hull to make sure they were all nicely in line before drilling through with a 2mm dia. drill, (**Fig. 5.15**). Even then, I chose to drill one port on the lower row with a 6mm dia. hole and look through as a final check on the position before opening out to required dimensions.

Fig 5.13 The lower bulwark rails to the forecastle. Note the dowels through to the supporting blocks below.

Fig 5.14 The bulwark rails finished and capped. The semi-circular rails around the tops of the round houses needed to be painted in order to disguise the white wood provided in the kit.

**Fig 5.15** **The positions of the gun-ports should be checked using the template provided and adjusted if necesary before drilling the 2mm diameter holes.**

## Cutting and Lining the Gun-Ports

There were three distinct types of gun-port to be cut. The two lower gun-decks had ports that had to be lined and fitted with port lids. The main deck also had rectangular ports but slightly smaller in dimensions to accept cast port surrounds. The quarter-deck and poop deck had circular ports into which were fitted wooden rings. The same size rings were also fitted into the rails of the forecastle deck. Note that there is an error on the pictorial view of Drawing Sheet 4 in that there are only four circular ports shown on the quarter deck - there should be five. The different types of gun-port are shown in **Fig.5.16**.

I first made up a 12mm square gauge with a 2mm dia. pin in the end. This was inserted into each of the gun-port pilot holes in turn and, with the gauge held tight against the side of the hull, the outline of each port was marked with a pencil. In order to attain a snug fit against the hull, the end of the gauge had to be angled differently for each row of ports. Each port was opened out first with an 8mm dia. drilled hole, then cut to almost finished size with a scalpel. I have a 10mm wide abrasive tool made up from a Perma-Grit strip which is ideal for finishing to gauge size. This method ensures that all ports are the same size and by starting each one with the 8mm drilled hole, there is ample scope to maintain accurate alignments along each row.

The gauge size for the upper row of square ports should be adjusted to suit the size of the locating spigots on the rear of the cast gun-port surrounds provided in the kit. It should also be noted that since these ports are visible on the inner sides of the bulwarks, extreme care is needed to ensure that the lining of the bulwarks is not split out as drills break through. For this

reason it is not wise to try and drill the circular ports to finished size, but trim with a scalpel or use a drill-mounted burr.

Each port on the lower two rows has then to be lined, first on the sides then at top and bottom, with 3 x 0.5mm strip. I tried to keep all of the inner edges aligned and, when the glue had set, the linings were painted red before the outer edges were sanded flush with the outside surface of the hull.

## Initial Painting

A light pencil line to indicate the position of the various lengths of brass trim was all that was needed at that stage before painting the several areas of upperworks light blue. I used Humbrol Acrylics throughout and No.5025 provided just the right shade of blue as a background to the forthcoming decoration.

The lower hull was painted matt white with a rub down between two or three coats. This was then masked off and the black area above the waterline painted. Almost certainly, that bearing in mind the amount of work still to do on the hull, the white underside will need a further coat later on. The hull with its first coat of paint is seen in **Fig.5.17**.

## Gun-port Lids

Several points to be made here. First, the hinges were painted before assembly to the port lids. I used epoxy adhesive to stick them in place before drilling the holes for the eyebolts. Although the instructions indicated that the lids should be fitted to the hull at this stage of the proceedings, I reckoned that with the amount of work still to be done on the hull, they would be rather vulnerable. I therefore put the lid assemblies to one side for later fitting after painting the undersides red.

One adverse comment about the kit. The two wooden parts of each lid came from a laser cut sheet. Unfortunately, the choice of wood is far too light. Thus, you have the task of trying to stain the top surface of the lids to match the hull planking or, alternatively, make up the lids from appropriate size strip from your scrap box.

## Brass Decoration

The stage had now been reached where some of the decorative pieces needed to be added. A couple or so points to watch here will make for a better job and avoid damaged fingers.

The decoration fell into two main catagories: brass castings, which were extremely well produced with little to do apart from filing the odd blemish from the back surfaces to ensure correct seating, and an etched brass sheet. The latter could be readily cut with a small pair of scissors, but extreme care was needed because the edges so produced were very sharp. I found that having removed one piece, it was best to deburr the edges straight away and gently coerce it back to a flat state. Painting the etched recesses with the appropriate colour, followed by cleaning the raised surfaces can be done either before, or after, cutting out. I did mine before cutting and everything seemed to work very well.

The stern gallery balustrading was cast in a more malleable material and, with care, could readily be bent to the shape required. However, I did find that, bearing in mind the com-pound curves involved, matters were eased by cutting through the bottom rail at three or four points, particularly on the outer pieces.

Holding them in place while the adhesive set is easy enough on the upper gallery where small crocodile clips could be applied to the ply-planked deck. The lower gallery was a different kettle of fish and I found that the most satisfactory way was to drill three or four holes just below deck level, to take the noses of the clips. These holes were subsequently filled before fitting the brass trim around the lower edge of the balustrading.

The decorative discs and intermediate leafwork around the hull below the lower gallery needed careful marking out and a little bit of coercion to contour the pieces to fit snugly against the surface to which they had to be glued.

Several of the brass items featured coats of arms. Rather than leave these pieces totally brass-coloured, I chose to paint the shield quarters red and white with the various devices later rubbed to expose the brass below. This tended to add small, but colourful details, particularly to the fore and aft sides of the upper works of the hull.

The various types of brass and cast decoration are featured in **Figs. 5.18, 5.19 and 5.20**.

## The Head Rails and Bow Structure

This part of the model tests the builder's woodworking skills probably more than any other part of the construction. Working from the lower details upwards, I first shaped the

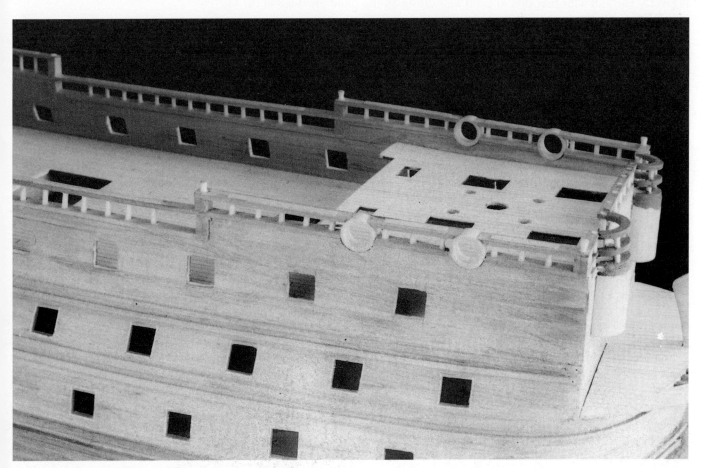

**Fig 5.16  The three different types of gun-port.**

**Fig. 5.17 The hull with first coat of paint and sitting on the stand provided in the kit.**

port and starboard cheek blocks that fitted between the bow planking and the stem. The shape and attitude of the outer face had to be taken from the curves of the etched brass trim that runs from the hull and up the stem to the underside of the figurehead. The angular and curved seating faces of these two blocks made it impossible to establish datum faces from which to work.

You may find, as I did, that it was helpful to increase the thickness of the blocks provided. Having done that, I proceeded to shape the two angular faces for seating against the hull and stem. The etched brass trim was then offered up and its outside edges marked on the outer surface of the block. Having made an allowance for the width of the decoratative brass strip either side of the trim, the top and bottom of the block was then shaped. The block was then permanently fixed in place and the trim and brass strips added. Again see **Fig.5.18**.

The brackets between the stem and the underside of the beak deck were then made up, ensuring that they were symmetrically and vertically fixed between, and to either side of, the gammoning holes.

The head rails were made up from decorative brass strip. There are three per side and, obviously, had to match port to starboard. The coat of arms each side of the fore deck were drilled and fixed securely in place, as was the ornamental casting at the head of the prow behind the figurehead.

I then made a card template showing the lines of the three rails and the separation between them. This was done by tracing the shapes from the side view of the relevant drawing sheet on to thin card. A little bit of technical adjustment was

needed here or, in the terms of the layman, cheating. By careful measurement from the model, I plotted on to a separate sheet of paper, the actual relative positions of the three fixing holes in the coat of arms and the casting at the top of the prow. The card template was cut in two and the ends re-positioned on to the paper and stuck down. The extended template was then trimmed to the outer edges of the top and bottom rails and offered up to the model for a final check. Any further adjustment needed could be made by cutting and retaping the template, (**Fig.5.21**). It was important to note that the four cast head timbers each side were identical and thus the separation of the rails needed to be carefully maintained.

## The Dummy Gun Barrels

Just a couple of points here. If, as I do, you want all the barrels to stick out from the side of the hull by about the same distance, then you will probably find that the previously-mounted support blocks won't do it. The adjustment needed was either to mount one or two small washers on the spigot at the rear end of the barrel to extend them further or, to drill a 6mm dia. hole through the block to house the main body of the barrel for those that protrude too far. Either way a small diameter hole to take the spigot should be drilled first at all positions.

The second point is to remember to paint the bores of the barrels black before assembly. I just dobbed acrylic paint inside, then wiped off the excess with a damp cloth before the paint dried. Once all guns had been put in place, the gun-port lids were put in place. Two small holes were drilled in the side of the hull for the ropes that made up the gun-port tackle. The ends of the required size of thread were coated with cyano-acrylate adhesive and inserted into the holes then tied off to the rings in the top of each lid and trimmed close.

## Deck Rails

There is not too much to say about the construction of these items apart from the fact that the top and bottom parts of each rail were made together so that any holes accurately lined up. All lengths were taken from the actual model rather than the drawings, heights, of course, were largely governed by the length of the wooden columns supplied.

## The Spiral Staircases

The method of construction indicated on the drawings basi-cally worked quite well although I made one change to the procedure for making the outer casing. This was made up of two layers of 0.5mm thick strip laminated together. The inner 3 x 0.5mm strips were held in place around the length of 32mm dia. tubing provided in the kit with two elastic bands. White PVA glue was then well rubbed in all over the outer sur-face and left to dry. This avoided gluing the strips to the tube proper which would have made the later task of cleaning up

the inner face much more difficult. The outer layer of plank-ing, 4 x 0.5mm was then added, again using the elastic bands to hold everything in place until the glue was thoroughly set. I saved myself a bit of time by making the lengths of the strips such as, with care, to cut three matching pairs from one assembly.

The dimensions for the heights of this outer stair shell were taken from the model ignoring those quoted on the drawings. The height between the related decks was critical and the sweep around the curve made 120º - the 42mm dimension quoted on the drawing not being attainable anywhere across a 36mm diameter circle!

The steps themselves filed to shape and the supporting dowel cut to a length matching the distance from the upper surface of the lower deck concerned to the top surface of the upper deck. The steps were overlapped by half their area and built up on to the dowel support. This procedure provided the the right degree of twist to the staircase. The manufacture and assembly of these various stages are shown in **Fig.5.22**.

The outer shell was then glued in position, and the various supporting strips, posts and rails added.

## Balustrading

The instructions and drawing showing the construction of the balustrading were quite effective although at first sight appeared

**Fig. 5.18 The brass decoration on the stem and round houses with cast items at the side of the forecastle deck.**

**Fig. 5.19 Brasswork and castings on the transom plates.**

to be a bit complicated. The main thing was to be absolutely certain that the top and bottom rail of each section were shaped and drilled together to make them identical. Corner columns were dowelled for strength and when adhesive had set the intermediate, undowelled columns were slipped into place.

## Deck Guns

These really needed to be made and put in place before proceeding with other deck fittings and equipment. In fact, those under the poop and quarter decks were impossible to place if the various pin racks around the mizen and main masts had been in position. Similarly, the two forward-facing guns under the forecastle deck need to be positioned before putting the hatch gratings in place.

The gun carriages comprised laser-cut side pieces mounted on pre-cut axle blocks, (**Fig.5.23**). The fit is a bit sloppy and I found that it was worth making up a little jig from scrap to help with proper and identical assembly, (**Fig.5.24**). I also used cyanoacrylate adhesive for a more instant grab. Carriages were

sometimes painted or often left natural wood. Unfortunately, the choice of wood in the kit for the various parts was a bit of a mish-mash and I therefore painted them, after assembly, dark brown. The finished assembly is shown in **Fig.5.25**.

There were a couple of traps for the unwary. The axle blocks for the front and rear of the carriages were of slightly different length as were the associated brass axles. The larger wheels go at the front and the smaller ones to the rear to accommodate the deck camber. Again the bores of the cannon barrels were painted black.

## Hatch Gratings

There were eleven gratings to make up from the parts provided in the kit, one of which needed to be cut into two pieces, (**Fig.5.26**). There were just enough pre-formed strips supplied, so there was no room for error. A new scalpel blade at this juncture was seen to be a wise move. The actual construction was quite straightforward, and I remembered to get the ledges and battens the same way round, fore and aft, on all gratings. I made sure, too, that the forward-mounted guns under the forecastle deck were in place before I assembled the forward gratings.

## Deck Fittings

Pin rails, bitts, capstan and belfry were all quite simple to make. On the pin rails there were a lot of pieces that were identical and these were made up at the same time. Nearly everything needed to be dowelled to the deck for strength particularly those items that would later have to take the strain of rigging.

The ship's lanterns were standard Panart pieces which I enhanced by lining the inside of the body with clear acetate sheet. Mounting them required quite a bit of patience to set them at the correct angle and height, but when finally positioned, they certainly looked very nice.

The anchors are the usual kit assemblies, with the stocks being provided from laser-cut ply. These did not look very impressive and really must either be painted or replaced with items made from proper wood. Anchor rings should be puddened for that extra professional touch.

## The Chainplates

I felt some disappointment when I came to put on the lower deadeyes and chainplates. Whereas many wooden pieces of complex shape had been provided as pre-cut parts, apart from the preventer links, deadeye straps and all other linkage for the chainplate assemblies had to be made up from brass wire. This in turn involved making a couple of little fixtures in order to attain some semblance of sameness throughout. Most model makers could handle this I don't doubt, but I do wonder why, in a kit of this standard, pre-shaped straps and links were not supplied.

The assembly to the sides of the hull was more of a problem than the actual manufacture of the bits. Tools have to come uncomfortably close to protruding gun-port lids and, even having drilled holes to take the pins that secured the lower end of the preventer links, pushing, punching or tapping the pins home was quite hazardous. Not a job to be rushed or attempted if you are not feeling in the right frame of mind.

The brass wire and preventer links are, of course, not the right colour and should be painted. I painted mine after assembly together with the deadeyes.

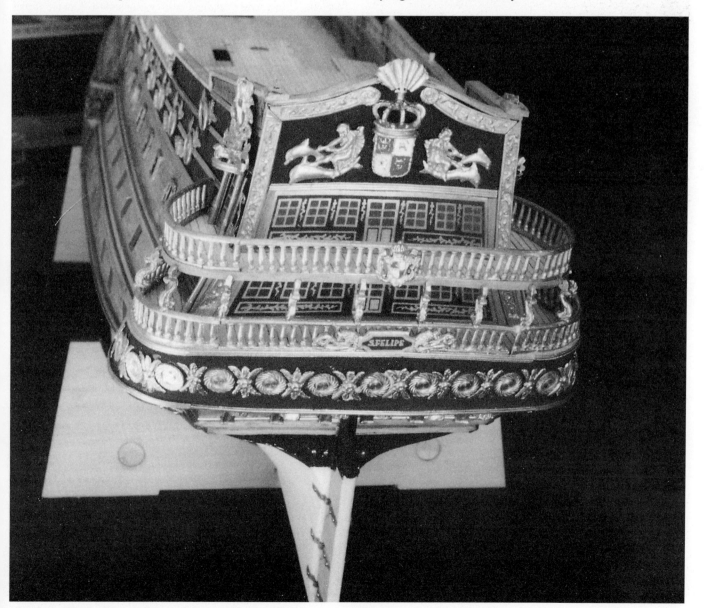

**Fig. 5.20 The ballustrading and decoration around the stern galleries.**

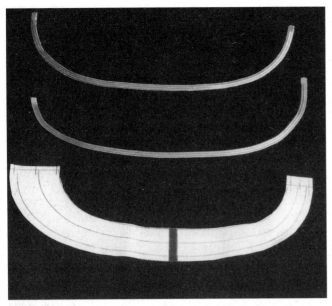

Fig. 5.21 The paper template for the head rails. May be used for both port and starboard - just remember to turn the brass strip face down for the opposite band!

The deck fittings and chainplates are shown in **Figs.5.27, 5.28, 5.29, and 5.30**.

## The Stand

Up until now, I had used the dry-assembled stand parts provided in the kit in order to support the hull during construction. As I got nearer to completion, I felt that the model

Fig. 5.22 The various stages of construciton for the carcases of the spiral staircases. Make the cylindrical stage long enough, and it will provide for three matching pairs.

deserved something a bit better than the dowel/ply plate stand given. Even when stained and varnished it looked rather crude, so I resorted to using a suitably-sized house nameplate and a couple of turned pedestals.

## Masts, Spars and Rigging

This was one model that was just too big to comfortably house at home and I reluctantly had to build it in the hull-only format. However, for the purposes of writing a fairly balanced review of the kit, I did study the ongoing instructions and

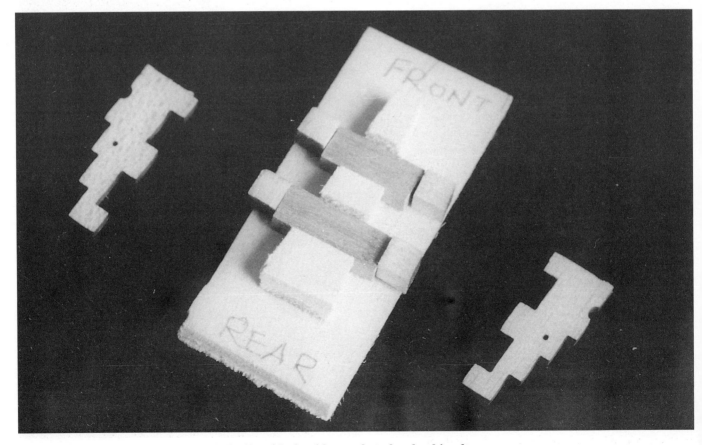

Fig. 5.24 The axle blocks in place on the jig with the sides ready to be glued in place.

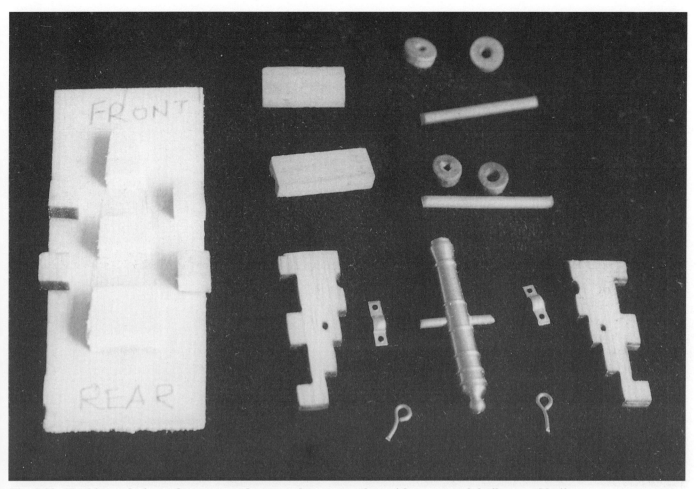

**Fig. 5.23  The bits and pieces that go to make up each gun, together with my scratch built assembly jig.**

drawings and quickly realised that the mast and yard construction would follow the usual kit procedures. In this instance, however, many of the mast parts such as cross trees and trestle trees, cheeks, etc. were pre-cut, the aim being; to make life a lot easier.

Rigging would not be too complicated on a model of this

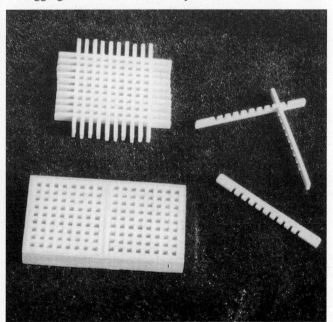

**Fig 5.26  One of the eleven gratings to be made, together with an assembled pair ready for deck mounting.**

size, albeit that there is a lot of it! Sails are not provided in the kit, so access for fingers and tools would be relatively good.

Having fitted stub masts and bowsprit to my model, I had only to add the gammoning from bowsprit to prow.

## Conclusions

Even at the price of nearly £600.00, you get your enjoyment at a very acceptable rate per hour. I don't like quoting the number of hours involved in making such a model, because it is difficult to define the capabilities and capacities of the average model maker, but you have to expect more than a few weekends to do the job. In any case, I am nowhere disciplined enough to keep an accurate tally of my hours.

Panart enjoy a good reputation for their kits but, as with all kits, you can find fault, and this is no exception. However, the majority of adverse comments would fall into the realms of nit-picking. My own feeling is that some of the parts would be better made from strip material rather than ply. Obviously, it was considered a better option to provide pre-cut parts in ply rather than ask the model maker to do a bit more work and fashion his own anchor stocks and mast parts, etc. I wonder? However, on the other hand, I felt that the kit was let down somewhat by the exclusion of pre-shaped chainplates.

The drawings were good, both pictorially and orthographically and the instructions were reasonably concise and detailed. From the little I know about Spanish ships of the period, the details of design and rigging looked pretty good. I

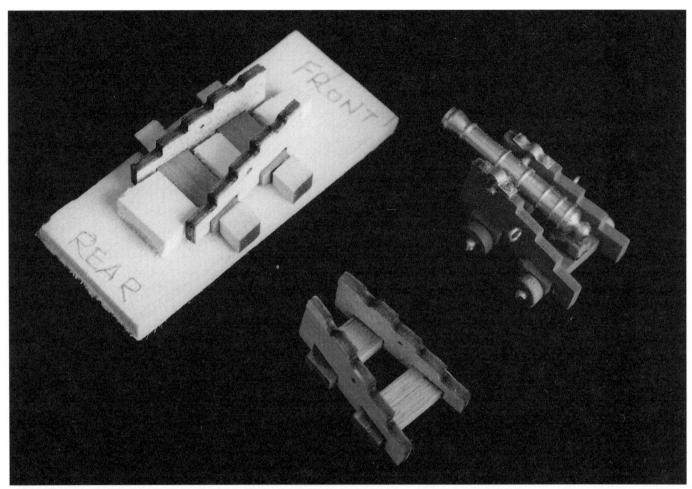

Fig 5.25 The completed carriage, on and off the jig and the final gun carriage assembly.

Fig 5.27 The fitted out rear decks. Note also the chainplates.

Fig 5.28  The deck area around the main mast.

Fig 5.29  The capstan and belfry.  The galley stack goes down through the main deck.

**Fig 5.30 The front end. Remember to pudden the anchor rings.**

cannot comment on accuracy with regard to the San Felipe per se, since I could find no readily available information on the vessel. I suspect that it may fall into the class of "Typical Mythical"! Nonetheless, you do finish up with a very impressive model and one which should give most modellers a great deal of satisfaction.

Value for money? In terms of the number of hours of enjoyment, and the final result, very good value.

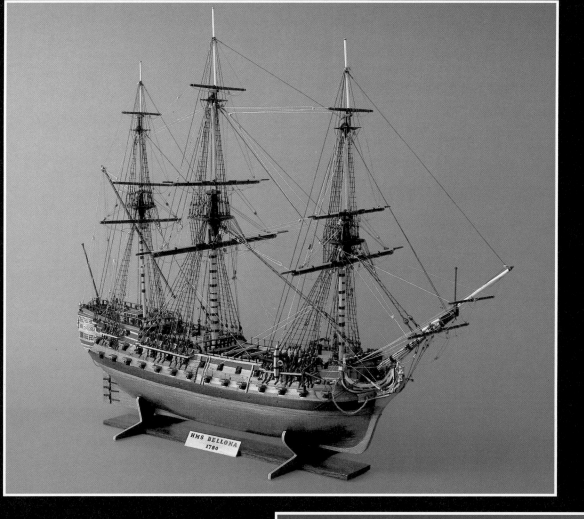

# The finished models in colour

**Above:**
*"HMS Bellona"*

**Right:**
*"HMS Unicorn"*

**Right:**
English Brig "*Portsmouth*"

**Centre:**
17th Century Spanish 104 gun
"*San Felipe*"

**Bottom:**
Sea Ewer "*Elbe*"

**Right:**
*HMS Bounty's* Jolly Boat

**Below Left:**
*"HMS Victory"*

**Below Right:**
*"The Pride of Baltimore"* 1988

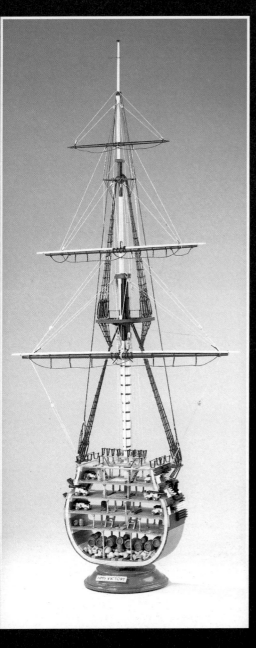

**Left:**
Armed Transport *"Bounty"*

**Below:**
The American Whaling Brig *"Viola"*

# CHAPTER 6

# *H.M.S. BOUNTY'S* JOLLYBOAT

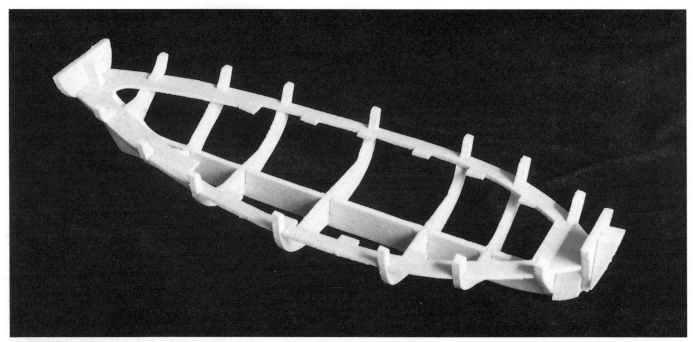

**Fig. 6.1 The frames located and positioned squarely on the keel and stem.**

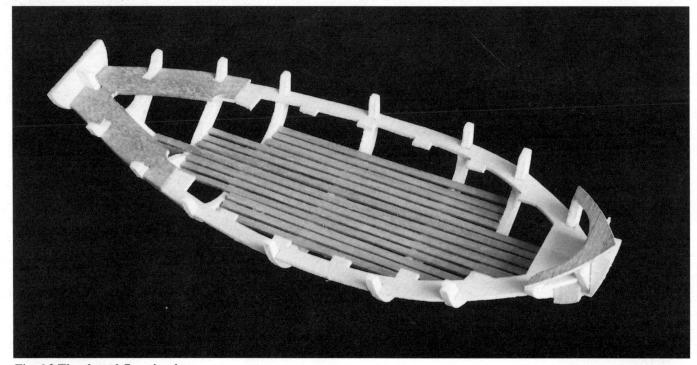

**Fig. 6.2 The slatted floor in place.**

Artesania Latina have produced a kit for this small craft obviously with the beginner in mind. The boat itself is typical of those carried by all sorts of vessels of the period and, even for the more experienced model maker, will make a pleasant change to the complexities of the larger vessels.

## The Kit

Drawings and coloured photographs featured on the box, complemented the written instructions and parts list, to steer the builder, stage by stage, through the construction of a model 415mm long and 360mm high.

The sheet parts were extremely well pre-cut and all materi-

al was of good quality. A sheet of cloth was provided for the sails and the kit contained all fittings required, rigging thread and parts for a stand.

Planks for the carvel sheathing were, where necessary, ready-shaped and pre-cut thus getting over one of the larger problems faced by the less experienced.

## Tools Required

A nice sharp modelling knife or scalpel, a small saw, a light hammer or pin-pusher and a drill to produce 0.75mm dia. holes were all that were needed for the making of the model. Two or three grades of sandpaper and a file for shaping the edges of the frames provided the abrasive requirement.

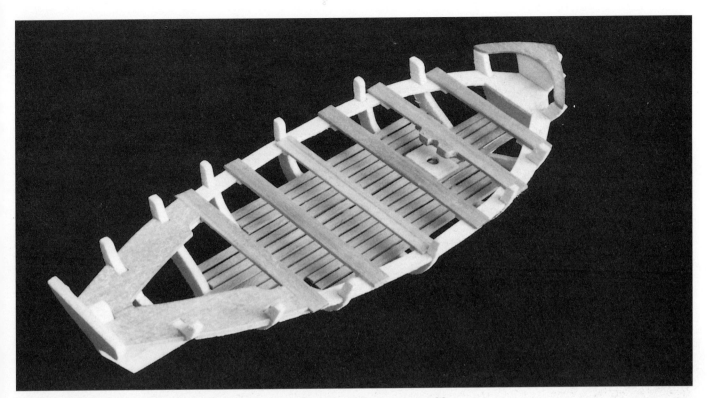

Fig. 6.3  **The thwarts and stern seats should be sanded smooth before assembly.**

White PVA, contact adhesive and a spot or two of cyano-acrylate performed all of the sticking necessary.

Paint and varnish were needed for finishing and, depending on your craftsmanship, maybe a small amount of filler.

## Building the Hull

All parts for the hull carcase were pre-cut and need little doing to them apart from removing them carefully from the sheet.

Nine frames slotted into a false keel and a "deck" piece nicely located everything in true position, (**Fig.6.1**). The inside edges of the frames and the deck had to be sanded smooth before applying adhesive because these surfaces are exposed on the finished model.

The inside bottom of the boat comprised a series of slats cut from strip to the sizes quoted in the parts list, (**Fig.6.2**). A scrap piece of the strip was used as a spacer to maintain uniform separation. It was found more convenient to sand the

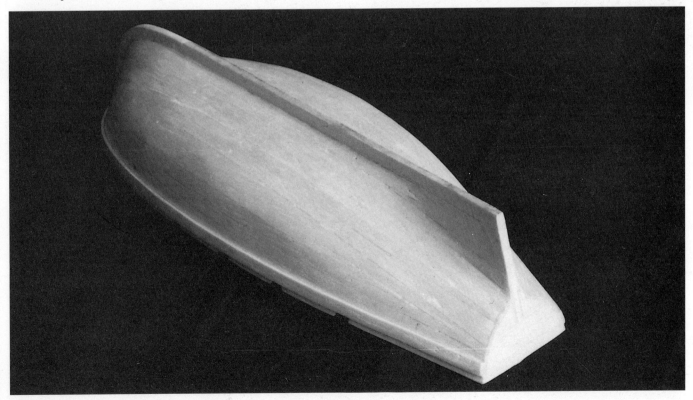

Fig. 6.4  **The completely sheathed boat.**

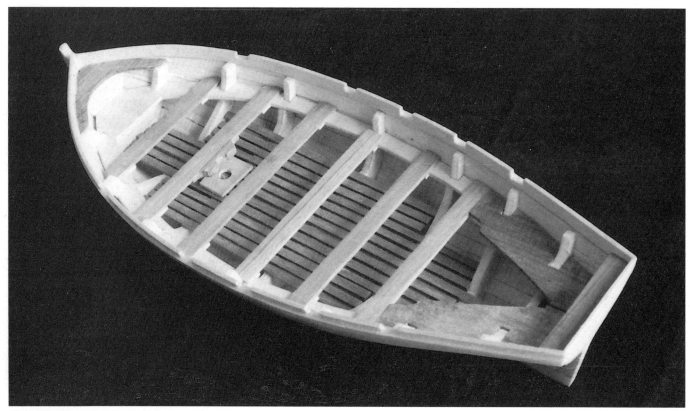

Fig. 6.5 **The top edges of the boat in place.**

strips smooth before fixing in place. Similarly, the stern seats and the thwarts were sanded before assembly, (**Fig.6.3**).

The planking started at keel level using parallel strips followed, at a higher level, with a combination of pre-formed pieces and parallel strips. Planks should be both glued and pinned to the frames. I found that the pins could fairly easily be pushed into place rather than hammered, ensuring that the heads were not sunk into the surface of the planks. If the instructions are closely followed, a fairly neat planking operation can be achieved. A few stealers, those wedge-shaped bits

that fill in the gaps between the planks at the stern, were required to complete the sheathing, (**Fig.6.4**). One point that is worth mentioning, particularly to the newcomer to the hobby, is that some of the inside surface of the planking will be seen on the finished model. Make sure that any adhesive that splurges out of the joints on the inside is removed before it dries; it will look pretty horrible if you don't.

The top edges of the planking were trimmed level with the tops of the frames and all the pins removed before rubbing down the outside of the boat to a smooth surface. Depending

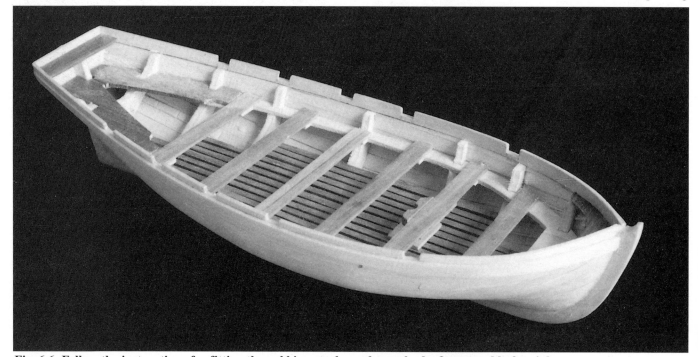

Fig. 6.6 **Follow the instructions for fitting the rubbing strake and top planks for a trouble free job.**

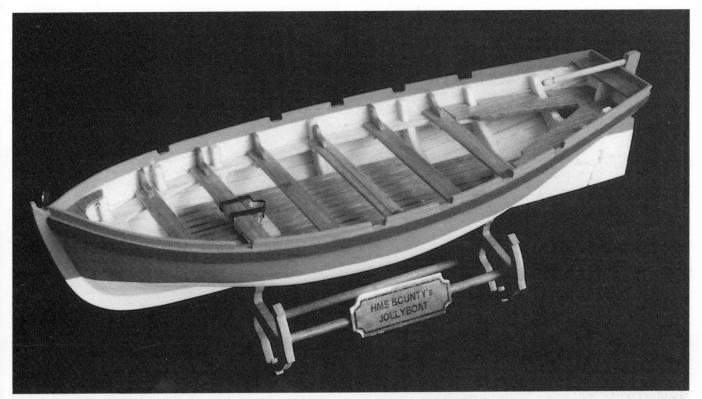

**Fig. 6.7 The finished hull. Note the knees on the thwarts and the fitting for holding the mast.**

on how good you have done your planking, some filler may be required to fill any small gaps that may have been left. The top edges of the boat were then built up and the slots for the oars cut in, carefully following the recommended procedure, (**Figs. 6.5 & 6.6**).

The remaining wooden parts were made and fitted together and the rudder and tiller put together. Before actually fitting the rudder in place, the entire outer surface of the hull was given a coat of sanding sealer followed by a finishing rub down. The rudder was then hung in place.

## The Stand

The simple, yet very effective, stand was assembled. It was made at this particular time in order that there was something for the model to stand on during the final stages of construction. The two pre-formed end plates needed a little finishing before joining together with a pair of dowel rods. A couple of coats of varnish should be applied before adding the self-adhesive nameplate.

## Finishing the Hull

With the boat seated on the stand, the position of the waterline was marked all round with a pencil and the first coat of white acrylic paint then applied to the lower part of the boat. This showed up one or two blemishes which were either filled or rubbed out before putting on the second coat. A very narrow strip of adhesive tape, about 3mm wide, was used to follow the waterline to mask off the white paint while the upper surfaces were painted. You need to use a narrow strip so that it more easily follows the contours of the hull without leaving little kinks for the paint to flow under. I chose to give the whole of the boat, both inside and out, a coat of matt varnish to seal and finish everything off, (**Figs. 7 & 8**).

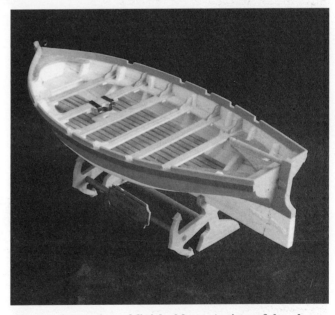

**Fig. 6.8 Stern view of finished boat. A piece of dowel was used instead of the brass rod provided in the kit.**

## The Mast and Spars

There is not too much to say about these parts, the drawings were self-explanatory, (**Fig. 6.9**). The tapering was easily done with a file and abrasive paper, filing first four flats to form a square section, then four further flats to give an octogon shape. The remaining corners were readily removed with sandpaper. A coat of varnish was brushed on then, when dry, gently rubbed down again before putting on a finishing coat. It was found helpful to tie on all blocks before assembling to the hull.

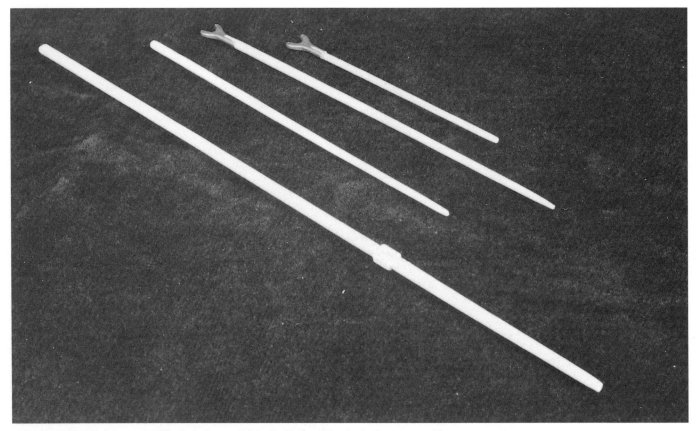

Fig. 6.9 The masts and spars. It helps to add all rigging blocks before assembly.

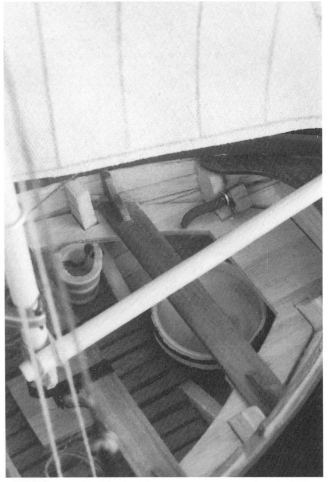

Fig. 6.10 A view forward showing the bowsprit lashing to the mast. Note the hand axe, bucket and tub.

## Sail Making

Circumstances have decreed that I have had to give very serious thought to the problem of finding an alternative method of sail making to the normal use of needle and thread. If, like me, you don't have this talent, then I offer the following alternative which gives acceptable results.

The first serious difficulty for one not adept at using a sewing machine, is the representation of all the seams that are visible on a sail. A line of stitches produced by a sewing machine is certainly speedy, but I can never seem to get the line straight enough and, unfortunately, when there has to be a series of parallel rows fairly close together, anything less than perfection shows up like a sore thumb.

A dark brown shade of ordinary coloured pencil proved to solve the problem quite well. Snags? Yes, you must use a chisel point and constantly keep it sharpened to a fine edge. Coloured pencils are, by nature, on the soft side and will not produce a thin line for more than about 50cm without attention to the point. It is also best to mark both sides of the sail.

The second problem is the hem all round the edges of the sail. Why have a hem at all? Answer - to stop the edges fraying, and again, there is an alternative to sewing.

Having got your piece of material marked out with the seams and outlines of all the sails, the next step is to apply a band of acrylic matt varnish around the edges of each sail. The band needs to be about 4mm wide and should encroach within the edges of the sail by about 1.5mm. The corners of the sails should also be well treated to provide adequate reinforcement for the attachment of blocks or rigging. Use enough varnish to ensure that it penetrates through the cloth. When thoroughly dry, each sail can be cut from the cloth and you

**Fig. 6.11 A view astern showing the swivel gun in place.**

finish up with a nice 1.5mm reinforcing edge all round.

## Rigging

The shrouds and stays should be set up first, making sure that the lanyards are correctly rigged between the upper and lower deadeyes. A smear of white adhesive rubbed in to the rigging thread will help lay down all those hairy fibres that seem to catch all the dust later on. This, of course, should be done before you actually set up the rigging. It also helps give that taut look without overtightening the lines.

It was important that the upper boom was lashed to the mainsail and the corners of the mainsail tied to the lower boom before rigging those items to the mast. That way, the correct angles of the booms relative to the mast were easily attained.

About the only serious criticism I found with the kit relates to the rigging. There was no belaying diagram and no pictorial or written instruction as to where the ends of the various lines were to be tied off. I chose to fit six belaying pins into the "deck" Part No.13 i.e., three each side, and slightly astern of, the mast.

## Conclusions

I found this kit to be an ideal project for the newcomer to the hobby. Apart from the belaying of the running rigging, the construction was well-illustrated in all its stages and the sequence in which to do things, well-thought-out. The timber was easy to work using the most basic of tool kits, the pre-cut parts extremely well-prepared, and the resulting model something with which any beginner should be pleased. The more experienced should not disregard this kit either; there is ample scope to do some additional research and come up with something a little bit special.

# CHAPTER 7

# H.M.S. VICTORY - MAIN SECTION

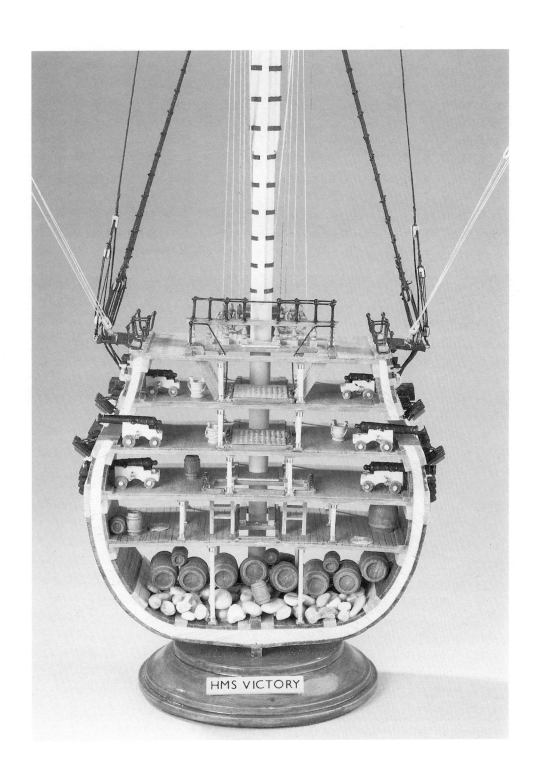

Fig. 7.1 The two part hull shell located on the building board by four angle brackets.

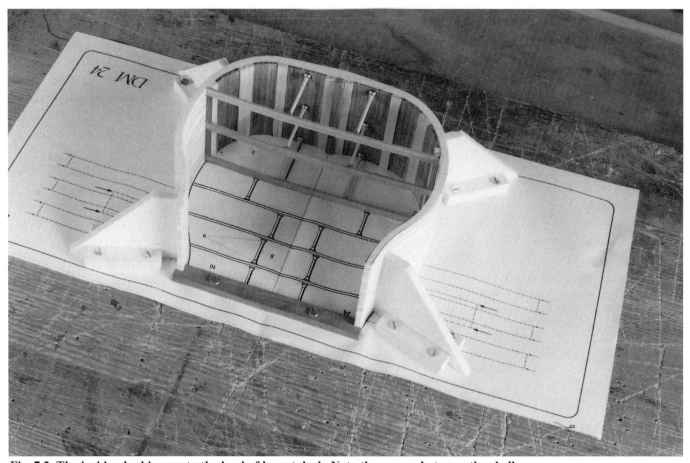

Fig. 7.2 The inside planking up to the level of lowest deck. Note the spacer between the shells.

**Fig. 7.3 The lowest deck planked with sides lined and beams added for the next deck.**

COREL have produced an extremely nice kit for this more unusual approach to Nelson's flagship Victory. It made a very pleasant change from the normal run of model ships and produced, at 1/96 scale, a hull section 60mm long, a width across the main yard of 325mm and an overall height of 715mm.

However, you should not get the idea that this is a sort of fill-in job between larger projects that will be accomplished in a couple of days. There were numerous aspects of the construction which were quite challenging, with close attention to the instructions and correct identification of materials being essential factors in the successful completion of the model.

## The Kit

As has come to be expected from Corel, the quality of materials and fittings was very high, the timber being accurately sized in section, fine-grained and straight. The main shell of the hull section was provided in the form of two pre-shaped halves, a first class and simple way to attain a strong and accurate structure.

Five sheets of drawings were well draughted and the multilingual instruction manual included a numbered parts list which directly related to both the instructions and the drawings. There were numerous pre-cut parts, a display stand and nameplate. Three different sizes of tan-coloured rigging thread completed the package.

The instructions gave clear advice that the quoted sequence of construction be closely followed and that even the more experienced model maker should not be tempted to deviate from them. This was advice not to be ignored.

## Tools Required

The usual craft knife and scalpel were adequate for most major cutting, a razor saw and David plane were also useful together with a light hammer and a couple of small files. A 12 volt electric drill with an assortment of drills up to 2mm diameter was needed and the normal assortment of abrasive papers. White PVA, clear glue, two-part epoxy and some cyanoacrylate covered all the adhesive requirements. Paints were also needed to provide the finishing touches. I used Humbrol Colour 103 for the ochre and Humbrol acrylic 5085 for the black.

## Building the Hull

Four alignment brackets were made from materials provided and, having positioned the relevant part of the drawing on a building board, the brackets were screwed into position to align and hold the two-part hull shell in place, (**Fig.7.1**). Having glued the two pre-shaped hull pieces together, it was recommended that the assembly was pinned in position around the inside edge. I found that a spacer bar between the uppermost ends of the shell was more effective, at least until the uppermost deck was built. It was recommended that the building board be mounted in the vertical plane for the construction process. I have to say that this felt a little bit awkward, but I stuck with it, knowing that it would undoubtedly be the means of keeping everything nice and square.

The planking on the inside of the hull was applied first up to the level of the lowest deck, (**Fig.7.2**). It was important to cut the ends of the planks that sat against the building board

Fig. 7.4 All decks in. Nothing was added to the top deck until later.

Fig. 7.5 The finished gun ports and main entrance. The outer edges of the steps were trimmed in situ to common thickness when glue had thoroughly dried.

**Fig. 7.6 A stern view of the completed basic hull.**

properly square and to ensure that they were hard down on to the board when gluing them in place. It was found to be helpful to rub down the side planking before planking the deck and fit eyebolts for rigging the guns. I didn't spot the need for the eyebolts until it was too late. Holes need to be accurately drilled from the outside and the eyebolts fitted before fitting the deck above. The deck support columns, beams and waterways were then added and the deck planked and smoothed off, (**Fig.7.3**). This sequence was then repeated for each of the five decks. The rails on the upper deck were not added at this stage, (**Fig.7.4**).

Gun-ports and the main entrances to the vessel were then marked in position on the sides of the unplanked exterior surfaces before commencing the outer planking. The planks were cut square at the edges of each of these openings, leaving only the central core and inner planking to be drilled through when opening out the apertures.

A couple of points needed to be taken on board before starting work on the gun-ports. First, a sharp drill had to be used at fairly high speed, but without too much pressure. Failure to recognise these points would almost certainly have resulted in the inner planking splintering as the drill broke through. Second, it had to be remembered that the line of the drill had to be truly horizontal and not square to the face of the outer planking! The holes were drilled close enough together to help with the removal of the centre part of each aperture, then the sides cleaned up with a bit of tedious filing. I made a 10mm square plug gauge to ensure that all six ports were made identical.

The basic hull assembly was completed by the addition of the steps up each side of the hull, (**Figs. 7.5, 7.6 and 7.7**). Each step had to be made slightly different to its neighbour in that the angle on the back face had to match that of the hull so that the treads were all level. I also made a small cutting jig so that the lengths of step in each group were identical. A light pencil line on the hull ensured that their vertical attitude was correct.

Before proceeding further, I decided to mount the basic hull assembly onto the stand. It appeared to me that this would provide a stable platform for the task of fitting out.

## Fitting Out

The placement of guns and port lids presented little difficulty. The pin rail on the upper deck must be very firmly secured and I chose to use a brass wire dowel in each post for added strength, remembering that some of the rigging had to be belayed to this rail and thus the joints at the deck would be under some tension.

The ballast in the bottom of the vessel was not provided in the kit and you have to find something suitable for yourself. A visit to my local tropical fish centre revealed a fairly wide selection of shingles for putting in the bottom of fish tanks. A handful of the appropriate size, mixed with a slightly dilute PVA adhesive was spooned into the basement area between two pieces of shuttering and left to set. The shuttering makes the job relatively easy and having lined the inner faces with a

**Fig. 7.7 A port side view of the basic hull.**

piece of polythene bag from the kit, the stonework did not stick to the woodwork. The barrels and kegs were pressed into place before the glue dried; this helped to provide a better

seating for them. Everything was left overnight before removing the shuttering, see **Fig. 7.8.**

## The Masts and Yards

Corel described this part of the construction as being the most delicate phase of the whole assembly. There really wasn't any more problems than with the masting of any other model of similar scale. What was required, was a total dry-assembly of all the mast parts before getting out the glue pot and a careful note made of the sequence for putting everything together.

The lower mast had to be tapered at the bottom and square-sectioned at the upper end. Flats were filed on the sides for the cheeks and on the front for the fish. Iron bands were simulated with black card strips applied after painting the mast, (**Fig.7.9**). The battens on the square-sectioned upper end are better put on after the assembly of the main top.

The main top should have twenty-one battens on its upper surface. These were not shown on the drawings and really the top did not look right without them. Again, strips of black card fitted the bill.

For the upper cross trees, Corel suggested that the timber strip be soaked in order to attain the required curvature. I found that the strip provided in the kit did not take well to this process and, like me, you might find it easier to shape the cross trees from 5mm wide stock rather than try to bend the 3 x 2mm recommended. **Fig.7.10** shows the various bits and pieces before assembly.

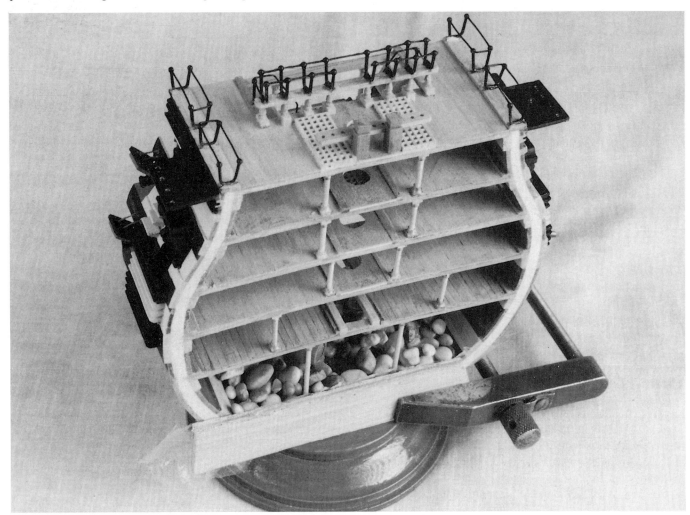

**Fig. 7.8 The hull mounted on the stand with shuttering in place for the ballast.**

Fig. 7.9 The iron bands put on the mast after painting.

Fig. 7.10 The mast, top, yards and stuns'l booms.

**Fig. 7.11 The main shrouds and backstay rigged.**

After everything was made, checked and dry-assembled, all parts were glued together ensuring that squareness and vertical alignments were as required. The assembly was then painted and put to one side.

The yards were relatively straightforward to make, the fiddly bit being the assembly of the strips that formed the centre octagonal section. I found that the choice of adhesive played a major part in this stage of the project, my preference being UHU clear adhesive. White PVA tended to warp the thin strip material being used, and cyanoacrylate was far too impractical, with more strips being stuck to the fingers than to the yard! The yards were painted before assembling the stuns'l booms and irons. The stirrups and footropes were added before putting the completed yards to one side while the standing rigging was put up.

## The Rigging

I like my standing rigging to have a tarred effect, so some of the thread provided in the kit had to be dyed black.

A considerable degree of licence has been taken with the rigging. With only a very short length of hull, many belaying points are suspect or non-existant. Obviously, there was a far greater number of shrouds than four to each side of the main lower mast, (**Fig.7.11**), although the six topmast shrouds are correct. Unfortunately, this does tend to make the rigging look a bit top heavy and the fitting of the lower ends of the futtuck shrouds a bit on the clumsy side. However, I guess that is something you have to put up with if you want to build this type of model.

The order of application given in the instructions was followed and the whole procedure worked quite well. However, I found one snag. The instructions certainly indicate which lines are belayed to the pin rail astern of the mast, (**Fig.7.12**). What they don't tell you is, in which hole! I rigged all nine lines concerned but didn't permanently belay any of them until I was sure that they all looked correct and balanced.

## Finishing Off

A few coils of rope and odd spars were added to the various decks as indicated on the drawings. The whole model was carefully looked over to make sure that there were no areas of paintwork that needed touching in or that no ends of rigging had been left untrimmed.

The nameplate provided in the kit was a plastic affair which, in my opinion, let the kit down. It really needed to be background painted and the raised letters highlighted which, at that size, was not the easiest task to do well. Accordingly, I chose to varnish a small strip of scrap timber and apply some rub-down lettering. A further coat of varnish to seal everything and I had a nice, albeit plain, nameplate.

**Fig. 7.12 Temporary belaying at the pin rail. Ensure that all lines are running sensibly before final fixing.**

**Fig. 7.13 The top and upper shrouds.**

## Conclusions

It is difficult to know what to say about a model of this sort. It is obvious before you even buy the kit, that building a short section of such a vessel, some liberties would have to be tolerated with regard to accuracy, so perhaps not one for the purist. However, the end result is very attractive and does not need very much space to exhibit effectively.

The pre-formed half shells certainly helped to produce a strong and well balanced hull section, although I wasn't convinced of the necessity for total construction on a vertically-mounted building board. Obviously, much would depend on your own depth of experience and craftsmanship, but I'm sure there are other ways.

The instruction manual tells you that it is possible to rig the guns. I have to tell you that it would be extremely difficult and, that much preparatory work, such us the fitting of eyebolts, would need to be done in the very early stages of hull construction. Even then, previous experience of micro-surgery would well prove advantageous.

As I said earlier, not a quick weekend job but, one where you can expend some one hundred hours in enjoyable model making activity. Currently, at less than ú65, one has to consider the kit as being pretty good value.

Corel kits are distributed by Euro Models, 35 Crown Road, St.Margarets, Twickenham, TW1 3EJ

Fig. 7.13  The completed section.

# *THE PRIDE OF BALTIMORE II 1988*

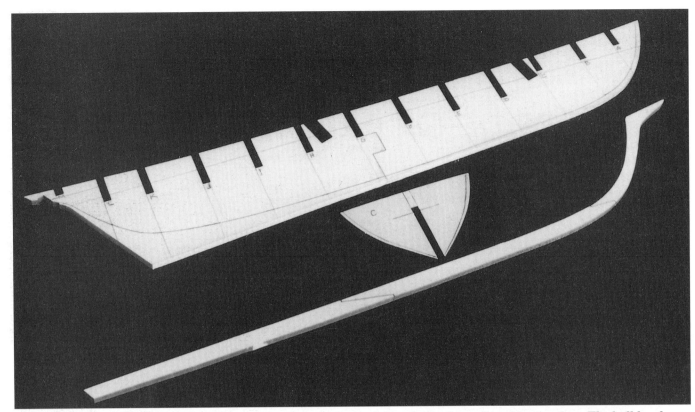

Fig. 8.1 The false keel. Note the bearding line defining the limit of chamfer on fore, aft and lower edges. The bulkhead was also marked for chamfering before assembly.

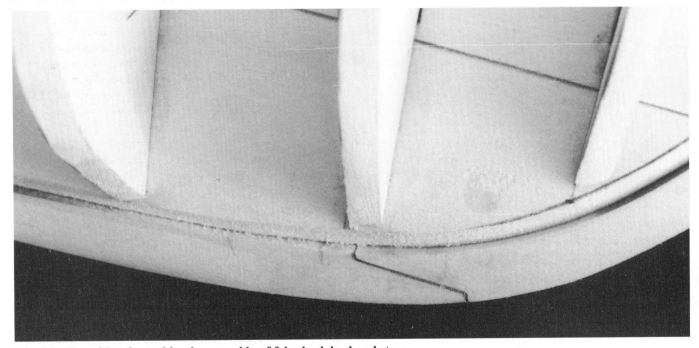

Fig. 8.2 The rabbet formed by the assembly of false keel, keel and stem.

The *Pride of Baltimore ll* was launched in April 1988, received full certification in January 1989 and has since sailed to many ports. Designed by Thomas Gillmer and built by G.Peter Boudreau, it replaced the earlier *Pride of Baltimore* lost at sea in 1986.

Built primarily as a means of providing public attraction to the Inner Harbour area at Baltimore, the design was based on the early designs of Baltimore Clippers, many drawings of which were done in Britain during surveys following the war of 1812.

*The Pride of Baltimore ll* was made as authentic as possible but with a few concessions to modern safety requirements, notably an auxilliary engine and feathering props. The ship also has a steering wheel instead of a tiller to conform to U.S.Coast Guard watch procedures and the foremast does not feature a fore course.

The hull is 108 feet stem to stern with a beam of 26 feet; Model Shipways kit produces a model 32in (812mm) overall length.

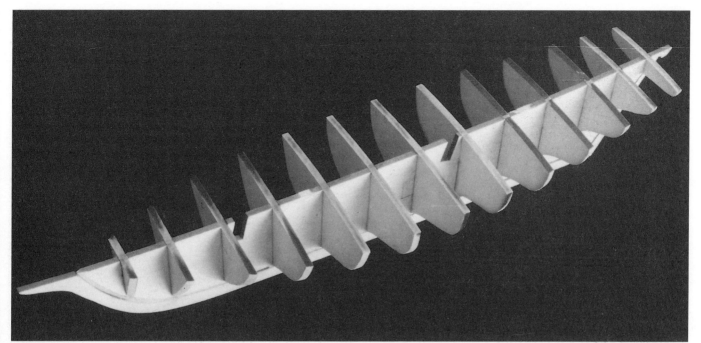

**Fig. 8.3 Assembly of prepared bulkheads.**

## The Kit

This being the first modern American kit that I had been presented with, there were several things that took my eye as soon as I opened up the box.

The first was the instruction manual, probably the best I have ever seen in a kit anywhere. Not only does it tell you what to do, but how to do it, with supporting illustrations and photographs of the actual vessel. Apart from the constructional stages, there were sections on tools required, painting, staining, soldering and how to get the best from the drawings - 48 pages of excellent guidance and information.

The drawings were clear but finely-draughted, three double-sided rolled sheets. By finely-draughted, I mean lines that are fine enough to take off measurements directly from the plans where necessary. The drawings were supplemented by a comprehensive parts list. All dimensions and wood sizes are, of course, in the imperial system rather than metric.

The major parts for the hull were laser cut in basswood, all strip wood was basswood, beech dowelling was provided for masts and spars and, the only piece of ply, featured laser cut mast hoops. There was a host of brass and Britannia metal fittings, walnut blocks and deadeyes, and four different hanks of rigging thread.

## Tools Required

The usual craft knife and/or scalpel, a selection of small drills up to 3mm diameter with pin chuck or 12 volt electric drill, small tack hammer and fine nosed pliers were supplemented, for this model, with some miniature carvers, chisels or gouges and a small soldering iron. A selection of medium and fine grit sandpapers and some needle files were also required. White PVA, cyanoacrylate and two-part epoxy provided all the adhesive necessary.

To make the model as authentic-looking as possible, paints, stains and varnishes were needed. The drawings indicated all the recommended colours. Obviously for best finish, primers and fillers were also used.

## Building the Hull Carcase

Although the basic carcase was a series of bulkheads mounted on a false keel, the method of construction adopted in this American kit was somewhat different to that used by the vast majority of European kits.

The false keel was made up of two laser cut parts, glued together, and left overnight to thoroughly set. Reference lines for the accurate location of the bulkheads were marked on both sides together with the bearding line, (**Fig.8.1**). The latter defines the limit of chamfer to be cut on the fore, aft and lower edges of the false keel. Its contour was taken directly off the drawings via co-ordinates at each bulkhead position. A craft knife and chisel were used to produce the chamfer, leaving a constant width of witness all along the edge of the keel as required. Keep your sharpening stone handy to maintain a high degree of sharpness on the edges of your cutting tools and you will find that basswood then cuts easily and cleanly.

However, it was at this juncture that I discovered an inconvenience that I haven't found with other timbers. The friction of sharp steel tools, cutting through basswood, appears to induce quite a static charge in the shavings. Consequently they stuck to clothes and shoes, in fact anything that had a man-made fibre content. Sweeping them up was also difficult because they stuck to the bristles of the broom, thus the vacuum cleaner had to be kept to hand and used at the end of each model making session.

The three parts that comprised the keel/stem assembly were glued together and kept flat while the two laser cut scarf joints completely cured, again see **Fig.8.1**. The attachment of this sub-assembly to the false keel provides the rabbet into which the subsequent planking is housed, (**Fig.8.2**). A similar feature is provided aft by the addition of the sternpost. Due to the small area of glue contact, several dowels were used for added strength.

The laser cut bulkheads were all identified and marked up with their locating reference lines before being removed from the sheet. Again, contrary to usual European procedures, the

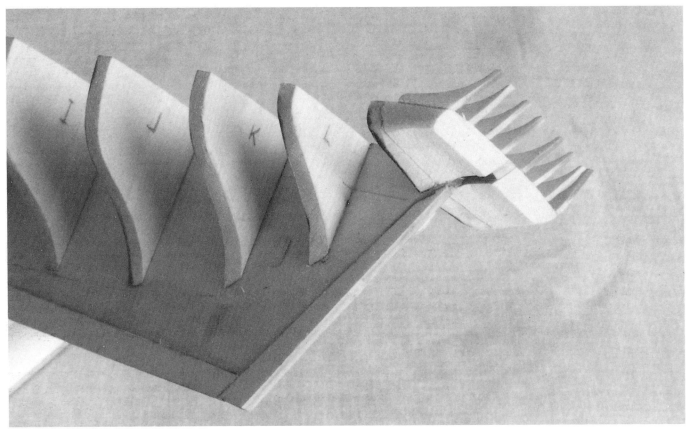

**Fig. 8.4 The carved stern blocks and transom knees.**

edges of the bulkheads were bevelled before assembly to the false keel. The amount of bevelling was taken off the drawings, the position of the bearding line being clearly shown. I was pleasantly surprised to find that, when the bulkheads were assembled, the edge bevelling and the keel chamfer below the bearding line matched up remarkably well, with little or no adjustment being required. The assembled bulkheads are shown in **Fig.8.3**.

Two filler blocks were then carved and placed behind the

sternmost bulkhead, (**Fig.8.4**). The drawings accurately defined the outline in all required planes and minimal blending with the bulkhead was needed after the glue had set.

The transom knees were next to be fitted, again see **Fig.8.4**. They are a little vulnerable during the ongoing construction and it was suggested in the instructions that a temporary strip be pinned across them to more securely hold them in place. Bearing in mind the size at the tips of these pieces, I felt that this was a bit optimistic and decided to immediately jump one

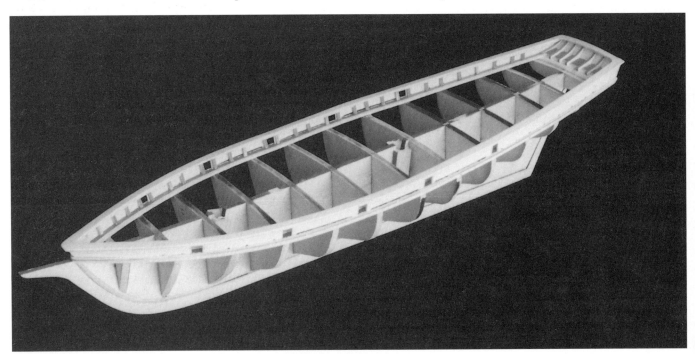

**Fig. 8.5 The stanchions and transom knees all supported by planking before shaping and fixing main rail.**

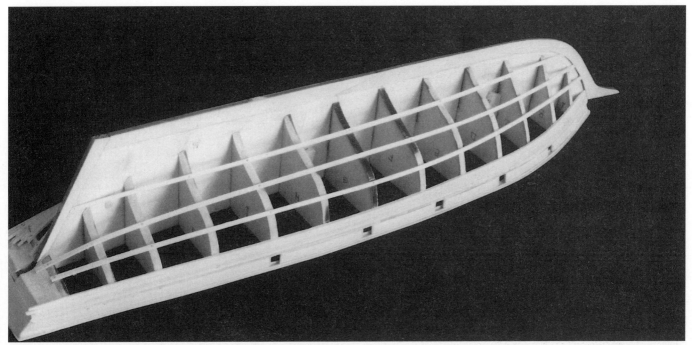

**Fig. 8.6 The hull framework sectioned up prior to planking.**

step ahead and fit the waterway across the stern between the knees. This provided a much stronger and permanent joint.

The port and starboard waterways were assembled, fitted and pinned in place while the glue dried. Before adding the nibbling strake and stanchions, the waterways were painted red. From now on in the construction you have to keep your eye open for desirability to paint as you go. It may seem a bit long-winded, especially as you may have to wait for two coats to dry before proceeding further, but it gives a better job and is worth the slight delay. Anyway, there are always things to make or assemble that will be needed later.

Fitting the stanchions is a bit of a dodgy job and needs a lot of care to get all the alignments correct. I fitted every fifth stanchion down each side and eyeballed the angles to coincide with the line of the bulkheads. The waterways and the stanchions are all very accurately laser cut and slotted and I found that these initial stanchions could all be glued in place with white PVA before gently pushing them into final position.

The suggested sequence recommended that the main rail should be installed next, followed by the hull planking. Like the transom knees, the stanchion/main rail framework was going to be very vulnerable during the planking process. I therefore decided to once again jump ahead, plank the bulwarks and cut and line the gun-ports, before adding the main rail, (**Fig.8.5**). This certainly provided a much stronger feature, less likely to come to grief during the ongoing construction. Another advantage adopting this procedure, is that the actual shape at the top edge of the bulwarks can be traced onto a card template, thus permitting the width of main rail to have a proper and constant overhang.

## Planking the Hull

The kit provided for a single-planked hull, although the option for double-planking was discussed in the manual, to the point where metric sizes and quantity of material were given, should the modeller decide to opt for a natural wood finish rather than painting.

The drawings provided an excellent guide to the sheathing stage of construction in the form of a planking diagram. It was recommended that planks be cut to 6" long which, although not truly to scale, conveniently puts butt positions relative to four bulkhead spaces.

The plank immediately below the sheerstrake (waterway) was applied first followed by the three planks that formed the main wale. The remainder of the area to be planked was then divided into four sections by the application of three battens, (**Fig.8.6**). It was important to carefully eyeball the line of these strips to ensure that their run was fair and identical, port and starboard. Each of the two upper sections was then filled in, using a small plane for tapering the planks as necessary for a nice snug fit.

The instruction manual recommended that the planks towards the stern be steamed to take up the more severe curves in that area. I opted to use try plank nipper, found it successful and used it throughout without any plank breakage whatsoever.

The lowest section involved wider planking material to produce spiled planks. Spiling is the development of the required shape for a plank to accommodate the correct curvature of the hull without trying to bend the plank on its width, i.e., edge bending. The instruction manual shows one way in which this can be achieved on the model in quite a simple manner. This is not an operation that I have come across in any of the European kits that I have built and, where spiled planks have been required, they have already been marked out or laser cut ready for application. In theory it is possible to geometrically develop the curves on the drawing board or computer screen, but it is usually far better to use an "on the hull" marking procedure, as described in this kit.

The entire hull surface was then rubbed down to a smooth finish, the transom fashion pieces added, then given a couple of coats of sanding sealer, rubbed down between coats. I then primed the hull with grey primer which, when sanded off, showed up any minor surface flaws which were then filled, (**Fig.8.7**).

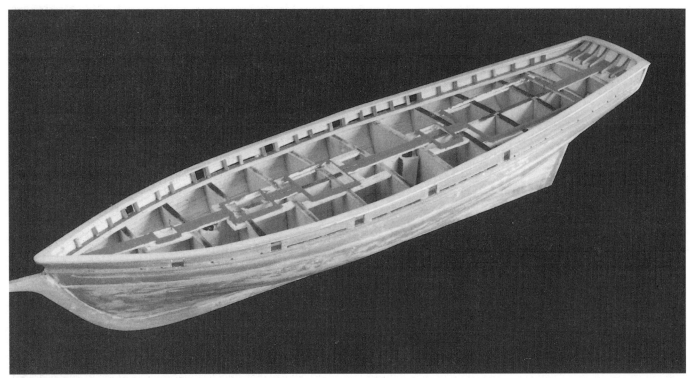

**Fig. 8.7 The planked hull with hatch coamings fitted and painted.**

**Fig. 8.8 The planked deck and painted hull.**

## The Deck

Before actually laying the deck planking, the hatch coamings were made up and painted. I made sure that the width across the outside of each coaming was a multiple of the plank width and that they were accurately centralised. This ensured that there would be no awkward fitting when it came to laying the planks.

The deck planks were blackened on one edge with a felt-tipped pen to simulate the caulking. This is the time your earlier accuracy in making the hull carcase comes to the fore, and you see whether the joggling of the planks into the nibbing strake is balanced, port to starboard. The edges were well-

glued so that there was no plank springing between the tops of the bulkheads, (**Fig.8.8**). This avoids problems when rubbing down and finishing the deck surface.

The stand, in the shape of the slipways used in Baltimore was made up at this stage, with the keel drilled to accept a couple of dowels. All timber is provided for the ways but not the main base board or the simulated stonework, (**Fig.8.9**).

Before moving on to the deck fittings and hatches, I did the main paint job on the hull using the Floquil paints recommended by the manual. These are fine-pigmented, spirit based, paints which provided good cover. Two or three coats gave a nice dense and hard finish, the paints being as good as any of the type that I have used in the past. Brushes do need to be

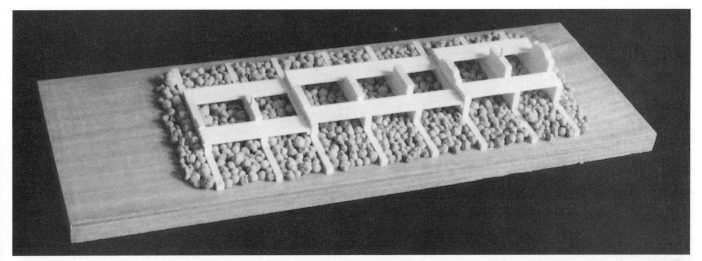

**Fig. 8.9  The stand. The base board and "rocks" do not come with the kit, the latter coming from the local tropical fish store.**

thoroughly cleaned with spirit cleaner to avoid later problems.

## Fitting Out the Deck

There was a wealth of small details to make and assemble, some to be fabricated from scratch and some Britannia metal fittings to be cleaned up and painted. This part of the construction was quite time-consuming. Each feature was treated as an individual project and marked off on the plan to ensure nothing was forgotten.

All parts were very clearly defined on the drawings with details of colour and position. I made up the various boxes and access trunks first, ensuring that they dropped neatly into the relevant coamings previously fitted on the deck. All parts were painted before final assembly.

The deck prisms, comprising brass eyelets and costume jewellery "diamonds", provided a very neat way of simulating the means of getting light below deck. Be careful though, the "diamonds" were awkward to get hold of and needed care in positioning. It was important not to lose any because there was only just enough supplied to do the job.

I have to say that I found the Britannia metal fittings something of a disappointment. The degree of flash was OK, and what there was cleaned off easily, but the mismatch between the two parts of the die was in some instances quite pronounced and, on smaller items, spoilt the part completely. The anchors suffered from underfill of the dies in the fluke area.

The fabricated parts like fife rails, samson bitts, riding bitts and binnacle, needed to be dowelled into the deck for adequate strength. The fitted-out hull is shown in **Fig.8.10**.

## The Masts and Spars

The bowsprit was an interesting project in itself, the main part being shaped from square sectioned timber. The centre portion, of octagonal section, runs into a circular section at the

**Fig. 8.10  The fitted out hull.**

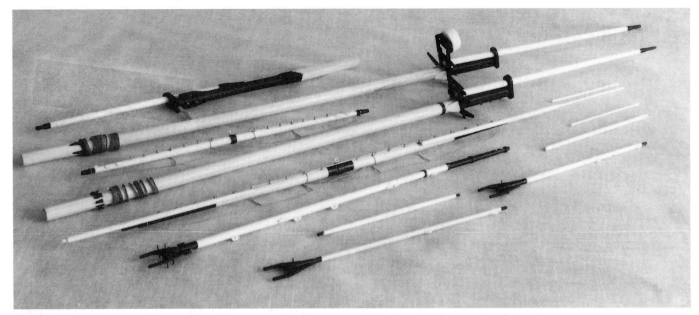

Fig. 8.11 The masts and spars. Consider mast rake when assembling tops to fore and main masts.

Fig. 8.12 The standing rigging completed.

position. The iron bands were simulated with strips of black card cut from the page of an old photograph album.

The jib boom was made and varnished then, when dry, the holes drilled for the rigging as required. The bowsprit was painted, then fitted with the necessary eyebolts before fixing the jib boom in place.

The fore and main mast parts were all made up, but I recommend careful study of the drawings before permanent assembly in order to establish a sequence of painting or varnishing and fitting together, (**Fig.8.11**). For instance, varnish and paint the lower mast before putting the mast rings on, and put these on before assembling the top to the lower mast head. A further point to watch for here is the rake of the masts, 13.5° for the fore and 15.5° for the main mast.

The yards and spars were all quite straightforward to make, the beech dowel rod provided being of excellent quality, making the planing and filing of tapers a trouble-free exercise. The major criticism that I had at this stage of the proceedings was that the kit did not supply the wooden beads for the parrals. Anyone who has attempted to make spherical beads of the small size required here, will know of the problems involved and probably opt to go to the store and buy some, as I did. I have to say that this was a bit of a disappointment.

Study of the drawings identified the positions of the various rigging blocks that, for later convenience, were best fixed in place before stepping the masts and assembling the spars. Note too, was made of several blocks that needed attaching to eyebolts in the deck which were also fixed at this stage before access became more limited.

## Rigging

As is usually the case, the standing rigging was the first part of the procedure. The shrouds and ratlines were put up followed by the stays to both masts, (**Fig.8.12**). You will probably find, as I did, that a little bit of extra tension was required on the backstays to overcome the natural twist in the cordage. With small deadeyes a fair distance apart, there was a tendency for the lanyards to twist so, as I say, a bit of additional pull was needed.

front end. A square spigot was cut, onto which was mounted the bowsprit cap. Flat seatings were made for the bees and the jib boom housing block which were then made and glued in

**Fig. 8.13 Looking down on the fore deck.**

I noticed too, that the black rigging thread was not fast-dyed and I soon finished up with blackened finger tips.

The bowsprit rigging was a bit fiddly due to the very small deadeyes and associated lanyards. It was found to be essential that each deadeye was checked to make sure that all of the holes were clear before they were attached to the relevant lines. The sail containment and safety netting below the bowsprit provided some source of strain on the eyes and this was done over several sessions to minimise the effect. A sheet of white paper laid on the bench below the bowsprit helped to keep the focus more comfortable. Alternatively, a trip to your local milliner's shop may reveal the odd piece of net used for ladies' hats which will fit the bill.

The running rigging is relatively easy to do, particularly if you remembered to tie all the blocks on to spars, masts and deck before assembly. The rake of the masts leaves considerable access to get at everything and allows the rigging to be tensioned up quite nicely.

One point that you may feel is worthy of consideration concerns the topgallant yard. It has no braces, truss or parral to keep it looking shipshape and hangs loosely on its halliard. I therefore decided to stow it, with sail furled, to the port side aft bulwarks which, the drawings told me, is the correct place for it when not in use.

## Finishing Off

Flags and sail material were not provided in the kit although complete details were shown on the drawings.

Anchors were rigged, noting that chain is used on the port side and rope on the starboard.

Coils of rope were made up and placed at the various belaying points as necessary.

## Conclusions

This kit was certainly different in its approach to construction techniques and really it is the level of the modeller's adaptability and craftsmanship that defines whether it is easier, or more difficult, than the European procedures with which we are more familiar. The pure carpentry content was a bit higher, but that should not present too much of a problem due to the high quality of the timber supplied and provided that you keep your tools sharp.

While full marks are in order for the quality of the timber provided in the kit and for the excellent manual, I have to say that the Britannia metal castings were something of a disappointment. The quality of the laser cutting was quite superb in the sheet material and a pleasure to work with.

The drawings were of a standard that would be ideal for a larger scale exhibition model. With the availabilty of the actual vessel for research and the co-operation of the *The Pride of Baltimore* Inc., the accuracy of the drawings should not be in doubt and certainly one couldn't have asked for much more detail.

As with many kits on the market today, there was only just enough of everything in the box. This is fine, provided that the very small deadeyes and blocks are accurately drilled and don't break apart when used, which is what happened in four instances with my particular kit. A bit of a pain if you haven't got suitable spares, and remember, this kit is to imperial

Fig. 8.14 **Looking down on the deck aft.**

Fig. 8.15 **The tops and spars. Note the rather severe rake on the masts.**

**Fig. 8.16 The finished model.**

dimensions rather than metric.

On the whole, I rather liked the different approach in the construction techniques but you do have to be adaptable and keep your eyes constantly on the manual and the drawings.

For what you get, I would think that it is pitched about right for price at £129.99 and available by mail order from Model Expo France BP 113-23 Rue Francois de Tessan, Ozoir la Ferriere Cedex, France or by toll free 'phone 0800 96 56 66.

# CHAPTER 9

# THE ARMED TRANSPORT *BOUNTY*

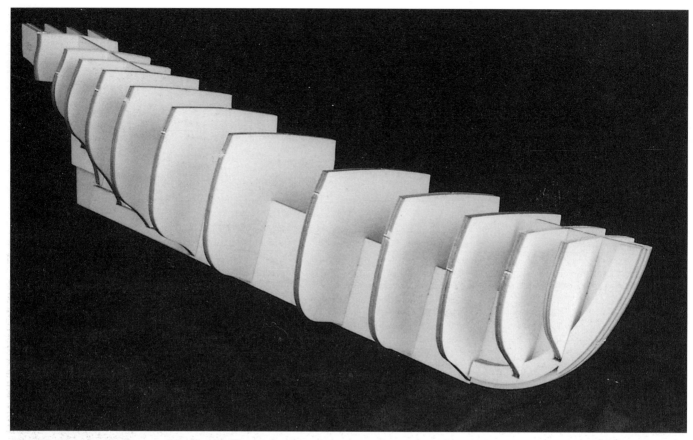

**Fig. 9.1 Frames in place on false keel with reinforcing pieces at prow.**

The Admiralty purchased the Bethia in May 1787. She had been built and completed on the River Hull some two or three years earlier, although at the time of her purchase she was lying at Old Wapping Stairs. The Admiralty Board were instructed regarding the vessel's fitting out and in June 1787, it was registered on the list of Royal Navy Ships as H.M. Armed Transport Bounty. Various changes were made to meet the standards of the day for the Royal Navy and in preparation for a voyage to the South Seas.

I suppose most people are familiar with the famous mutiny that took place in April 1789 about two weeks after the ship had left Tahiti bound for home. The ship was taken over and Captain Bligh, along with a number of his loyal followers, was set adrift in the ship's 23ft launch. Bligh, after a masterful piece of navigation, brought his small boat to landfall after a voyage of some 3600 miles. After his subsequent return to England, he was given command of a naval vessel and fought at Copenhagen where he was personally commended by Nelson.

Meanwhile, after several months at sea searching for refuge, the mutineers under Fletcher Christian, a former friend of Captain Bligh, finally ran Bounty aground at Pitcairn Island and burned her in January 1790.

## The Kit

First impressions were that the quality of the strip wood in this kit was excellent. All essential ply parts were very finely laser cut and the range of fittings was as high a standard as I had seen in any kit of this class. The drawings were supplemented by an illustrated instruction manual that was intended to give an extremely clear indication of what had to be done, and when. The manual's text was translated into English in a separate booklet. All in all, a pretty impressive package.

I looked particularly at the 1/60 scale quoted on the box and reckoned that, based on published figures for the vessel's length between perpendiculars of 84ft 6in, the actual scale of the model was more like 1/55. However, this did not really detract from the validity of the kit since everything seemed, basically, in proportion. You just get a model that is a little bigger than perhaps anticipated, the overall length finishing up at 760mm or, 30 in. in old money.

The kit was described as being of " Museum Standard". Exactly what this was supposed to mean, I am not sure. Certainly, the kit was capable of being converted into a model of such standard but, surely, that is more to do with the skill and craftsmanship of the model maker.

## Tools Required

The usual craft knife, scalpel and razor saw were the main cutting tools required. Flat and half-round files or Perma-Grit tools fulfilled the abrasive needs, backed up by various grades of abrasive paper. A small electric drill was most useful with a selection of twist drills up to about 2mm diameter, together with a light hammer or pin pusher. A plank nipper handled all plank bending.

White PVA, contact adhesive such as Thixofix, and a bottle of cyanoacrylate covered the sticking department.

There was a certain amount of painting to do, so surface preparation in the form of sanding sealer proved advanta-

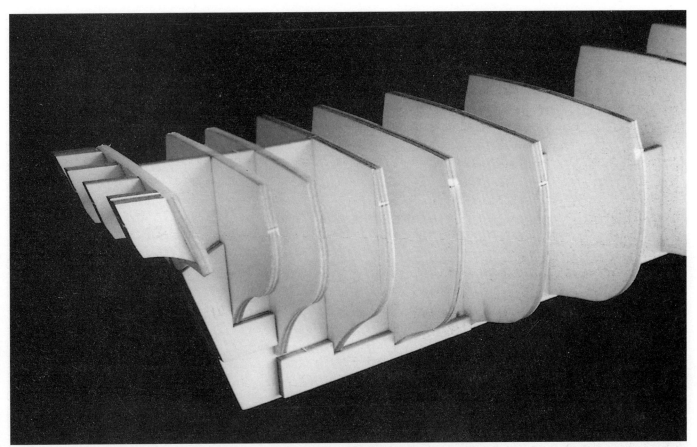

**Fig. 9.2  Assembled frames and stern reinforcements before shaping to lines of vessel.**

geous. As for paint, I tend to use Humbrol acrylics. When stirred properly, they cover well and don't get absorbed by the wood, as is the case of some other paint designed, perhaps, more for plastic surfaces. The other big advantage, of course, is that your brushes can be cleaned with water and maybe a touch of washing-up liquid.

## Hull Construction

The hull construction uses the frames on false keel method with reinforcements at stem and stern. However, right from the word go, there were one or two things that cropped up not mentioned in the instructions, or shown on the drawings, that might have caught the unwary or the beginner. First, it was fairly obvious that the kit had been updated to provide laser cut parts, which now combined together what formerly were several individual pieces. But, drawings and instructions did not reflect these changes.

The first job to be done was to cut two slots in the false keel to act as locators for the fore and mizen masts. I made these 8mm wide for the foremast and 6mm wide for the mizen mast, both slots being 3mm deep. The 6mm width was measured forward of the front face of frame No.13 and not as shown in the instruction manual.

The frames were a good fit on the false keel and needed virtually no work or adjustment to achieve squareness or alignment. I did, however, choose to angle the top edges of the frames to match the line of the deck before final assembly. The reinforcing pieces, particularly those at the prow, had to be trimmed for best fit. It is essential to glue these well and leave them to thoroughly cure before attempting to shape

them to the lines of the vessel. The assembled frames and reinforcing pieces can be seen in **Figs.9.1 & 9.2**. The planking of the false deck highlighted a problem with the 4 x 0.5mm walnut material. About 10% of the strips in my kit were tapered from about 4.5mm at one end to 3.5mm at the other. This was not the disaster first feared, since this material was also specified for the second hull planking, where the tapered planks could be accommodated. What is important, is that at the deck planking stage, you make sure that all the pieces selected are truly parallel. Any deviation would stand out like a sore thumb. The edges of the deck planks were blackened with a felt tipped marker pen to assimilate the caulking and Thixofix contact adhesive was used for mounting them on to the false ply deck.

The deck was glued in place before shaping the edges of the frames and the reinforcing pieces. The assembled deck gave the whole structure much greater stability for this somewhat arduous operation.

The transom and bulwarks are pre-cut from 1mm ply and it was here that I came across the first major problem. The width of the bulwark pieces should, according to the instruction manual, match the depth of the transom and be fixed to the edges of the rear frames. For some reason or other, the pre-cut bulwarks came about half width, thus providing only that part above deck level and with no fixing area whatsoever. Unfortunately, the sheet from which they had been taken was not large enough to cut replacements of the correct size. But, now knowing what the problem was, and because the pre-cutting had only penetrated to about half material thickness, the extra material could have been left on each part. Glue run into the lower edge pre-cut line would probably have given suffi-

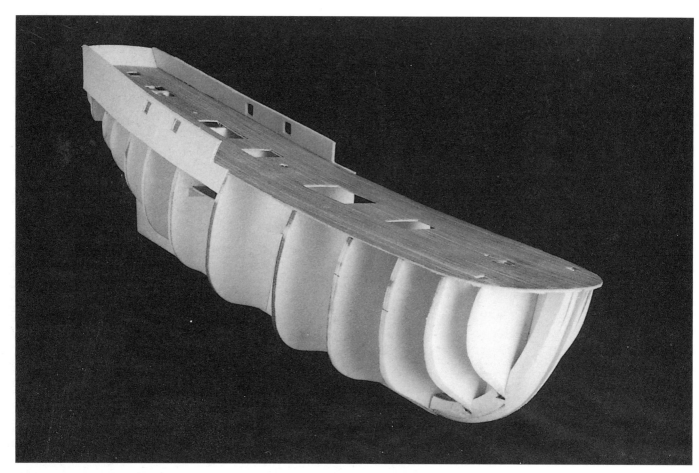

Fig. 9.3  Planked deck and bulwarks in position. The edges of the frames are shaped ready for planking.

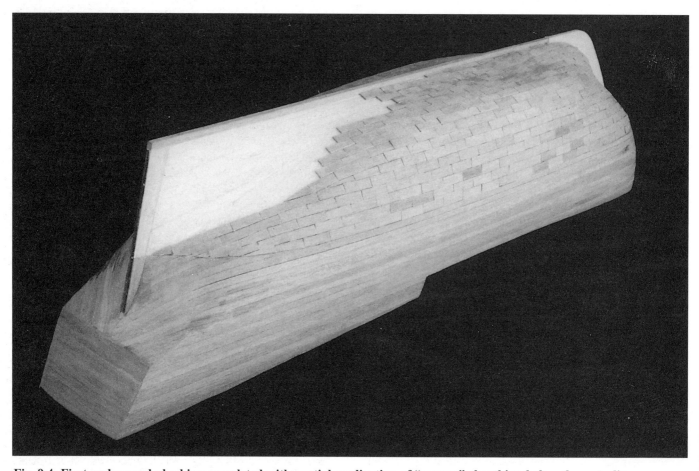

Fig. 9.4  First and second planking completed with partial application of "copper" sheathing below the waterline.

**Fig. 9.5 Rails and wales take longer than one might think. Careful measurements are needed to align port and starboard correctly.**

cient strength to work with since these pieces are ultimately planked on both surfaces. If, as I had done, you remove the bulwarks from the sheet before realising the problem, it's off to the store for some 1mm ply or plasticard! The assembled deck and bulwarks are shown in **Fig.9.3**.

The shape of the hull is not too modeller-friendly with regard to the first planking and, although I managed to do all bending with an Amati plank nipper, I found it necessary to thoroughly soak the timber first. Accurate marking and tapering were essential features of the planking process in order to attain a sound basis for the second planking. The difficulties with the first planking were compounded due to the fact that, in my kit, the timber provided was walnut. The type of material was not specified in the parts list, but no doubt lime or basswood would have made the bending task easier.

It further paid to study the shape and size of the transom, taking into consideration the etched brass and cast ornamentation provided for that area. A bit of careful measurement paid dividends later on in the construction.

The second planking, in 0.5 x 4mm walnut, was relatively straightforward and Thixofix contact adhesive was used throughout this stage of building. The curves at bow and stern still needed close attention and careful tapering was required to keep the planks flat against the surface of the first planking.

One point worth mentioning at this stage is the fact that Bounty would certainly have been coppered below the waterline. White stuff, as indicated in the kit, would not have proved adequate for a voyage to the South Seas. To simulate the plating, I cut the planking strips into short pieces, having trimmed the upper planking to the waterline, see **Fig.9.4**.

The capping strip that runs around the edges of the fore part of the deck is indicated to be made from 5 x 1mm strip. I

have to say that bending this size of material on the width around the sort of radius at the bows is ambitious indeed. However, all was not lost, the 1mm ply sheet from which the false deck was cut providing an easy solution. The material adjacent to the fore part of the deck was readily adapted to provide 5mm wide strips with just the right curve.

The main wale was made up from several strips of 2 x 2mm laminated together. Care was needed to ensure that the position of this feature was correct, particularly at the aft end where several other bits and pieces all come together. The drawings show a rubbing strake just above the wale, but I have reservations about this and believe that the upper part of the wale was actually a band of thinner material. Accordingly I used a couple of 2 x 1mm strips.

It was worth making up one gun carriage assembly to check on the position of the gun ports. It presents quite a problem if, when rigging the guns later on, you find that the barrels are too high to go through the bulwarks. Once the position was confirmed the port frames could then be fitted.

At this juncture, I decided to give the hull its first couple of coats of paint. I did this to make life simpler in the later stages of construction where wielding a paint brush amidst lots of fittings and protrusions would be a bit of a pain.

The 'midships rails and associated pin racks need to be glued and dowelled. They are a little bit vulnerable and certainly need to be strong enough to take the tension of the later rigging. The sketches in the manual are not compatible with the detail shown on the main drawing with regard to the assembly of rails to pillars, I chose the manual as showing the correct procedure.

The 3mm square strip for the pillars for the half-pounder swivel guns was painted before cutting each to length, again

Fig. 9.6 The basic hull construction completed and painted.

Fig. 9.7 The fitted out deck. The fife rails around the fore mast should be parallel to the waterline, not the deck. The head timbers are fitted ready to take the head rails.

**Fig. 9.8 The fitted out deck. The spindle of the ship's wheel should also be parallel to the waterline.**

to avoid fiddly work with the paint brush later on.

The hull construction to this stages is shown in F**igs.9.5 and 9.6**.

Having fitted the channels and boarding steps each side of the hull, I decided that further work on the hull would be made easier if the model stood on a stand. I discarded the one provided in the kit in favour of my own set-up. This is not to say that the Amati stand is inadequate, just a matter of personal choice. I also made up an oversize nameplate at this juncture, comprising a piece of thin ply, gloss-varnished, to which I applied rub down lettering. A further sealing coat of varnish was left to dry before trimming the edges of the nameplate to centralise the lettering.

## Fitting Out

There was a little confusion between the sketches and the photographs in the manual with regard to the direction in which the hatch covers ran, fore and aft in the photograph and athwartships in the sketches. Like gratings, I considered that the ledges would run across the hatch and the visible covers, like battens, would run fore and aft.

The windlass barrel was made up from a set of five castings. These fitted very well together into pre-cut wooden trunnions. To enhance the appearance of the assembly, I deepened holes in the barrel parts where indicated.

The chimney stack from the galley also came as a cast part. However, the stove fitted to Bounty was almost certainly a Brodie stove and, as such, would have had a circular-sectioned rotatable

stack. I therefore made the appropriate modification to the casting, retained the base part and added a wooden upper stack.

The fife rail assembly around the foremast proved to be a bit fiddly and care was needed to observe right and left handed supports as well as those fore and aft, heights having to accommodate the slope in the deck to bring the rails proper in to the horizontal plane.

The space between the uprights of the bitt forward of the foremast should be 8mm in order to house the butt end of the bowsprit. A similar dimension should be accommodated between the uprights of the knightheads adjacent to the stem. These features can be seen in **Fig.9.7**.

The remaining items were relatively straightforward and, treating each unit as an individual project, I found few problems. One feature that was missing from both drawings and manual was the binnacle. This essential housing for the compass should be positioned between the ship's wheel and the aft side of the mizen mast. My unit was made from scrap 5 x 5mm strip and the top surface faced with 6 x 1mm and can be seen in **Fig.9.8**.

All fittings were, where practical, dowelled and glued to the deck for maximum strength.

## The Carriage Guns

Bounty was equipped with four four-pounders and ten half-pounder swivels. The kit provides the complete carriages integrally cast with trucks and chock, requiring only the barrel to be assembled. However, as it was intended to fully rig the ord-

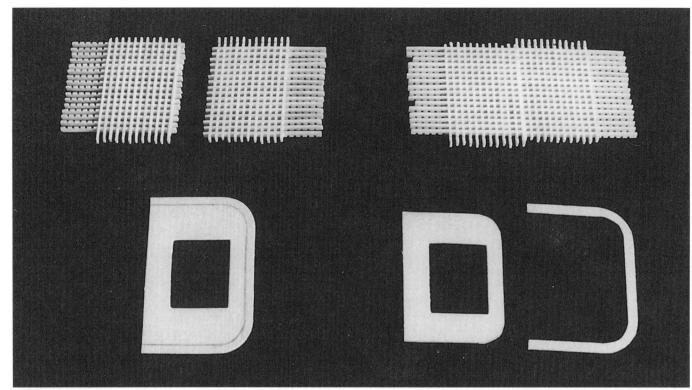

**Fig. 9.9 Two pieces of grating assembled then joined together. The pressed ply platform has been marked and cut to remove a 4mm wide band from front and sides.**

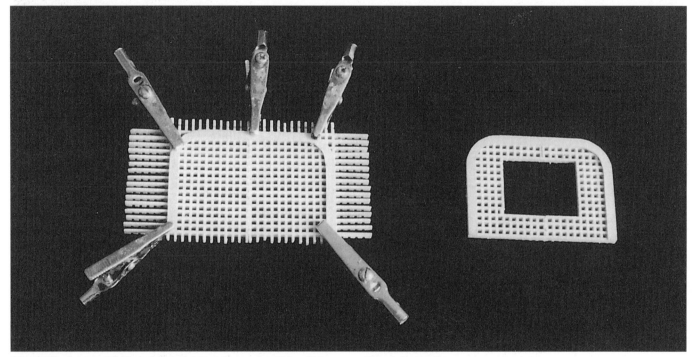

**Fig. 9.10 4mm wide band glued to grating assembly. Edges are then trimmed.**

nance, it was necessary to drill the sides of the carriage to mount rings to take the tackle. I chose to keep the rigging of the guns as simple as possible but, nonetheless, featured the breeching rope, the traversing tackle at the rear, and the gun tackle each side of the carriage to the inside of the bulwarks.

I am never sure that the results of rigging guns at this sort of scale is really worth the effort. It is extremely difficult to get a life-like appearance to the "hang" of the various ropes and I feel that in some ways this detracts from the overall presentation of the model. On the other hand, things do not look complete if the car-

riages appear to be free to slide willy-nilly across the deck. Maybe the fitting of just the breeching rope is an adequate compromise?

## The Head Rails

All parts came as soft metal castings, which added consider-ably to the ease of assembling items that are normally a bit of a headache. The cross timbers were put in place on the stem post first, followed by the rails. I found that it was best to start with the rail immediately below the cross timbers which

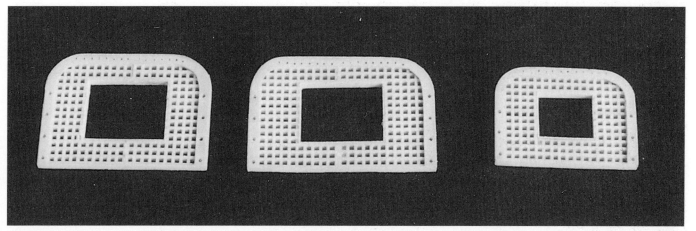

**Fig. 9.11  Centre cut-outs lined and the sides drilled for upper shrouds. Note the holes in the front edges for the crows feet.**

established a line for the bottom rail. The former rail was in two parts, the upper piece containing the scroll end behind the figurehead. The join was indicated to be just ahead of the front cross timber, but comparing the two pieces of metal, it was apparent that the sections would not match at this point. Accordingly, I made the join immediately below the scroll. The two upper rails were then added, it being found to be advantageous to start the shaping at the scroll end and then work along the length to the point where it was necessary to cut and shape the thinner end. It was much more convenient to do the total head rail assembly before putting the catheads in position.

## The Ship's Boat

Amati provide one of their excellent small boat kits within the main package and this makes up into a very acceptable part of the deck fittings line-up. A finely-cast shell is fitted out with wooden floor and thwarts, a little bit fiddly in places, but not too difficult to get a worthwhile result, see Fig.9.9. An in-depth review for this item in the Amati range of accessories has already appeared in the pages of Model Boats magazine. My only adverse comment here is that while the box art and manual photograph show two boats stacked amidships, the kit only provides one.

## Masts and Spars

I started by making and mounting the bowsprit. The construction was straightforward, the two main items being made from dowel rod, tapered and cut to required length. The bowsprit cap, together with the main and fore caps were provided in the kit as soft metal castings. These are fine for the two masts concerned, but some work is necessary to angle the two holes in the cap for the bowsprit, particularly the square hole for the end of the bowsprit proper. Some packing and, subsequently, filling was required to produce an acceptable result.

The little research that I had been able to do indicated that Captain Bligh had required the mast tops to be gratings rather

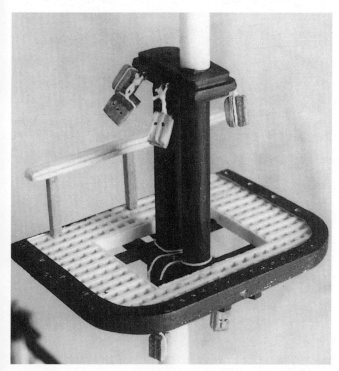

**Fig. 9.12  The fore top. It is most helpful to add rigging blocks at this stage having first ensured that all holes are clear!**

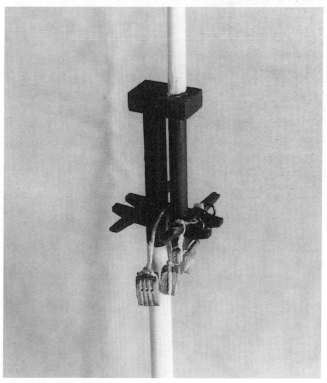

**Fig. 9.13  The topmast trestle and cross trees.**

Fig. 9.14 The completed standing rigging with backstays deliberately omitted at this stage.

**Fig. 9.15 The fore and preventer stays plus other bowsprit rigging.**

than planked. I assumed that Amati had also come to recognise this feature, and had included extra grating packs in the kit for the modeller to make this style of top, if he so wished. However, the drawings and instructions in my kit did not specifically mention such modification and I offer, in this review, the approach I adopted for their construction.

It was apparent that the gratings for the two largest tops would have to be in two parts, the mizzen top just fitting within the area possible with the grating strips provided. I then took the pressed out ply pieces supplied for the planked-style top and carefully marked and cut a 4mm wide band from around the two sides and front edges. The centre piece remaining was kept to act as a template for sizing and positioning the central cut-out on each top, see **Fig.9.9**. Having assembled two gratings for the main and fore tops, the cut-away 4mm band was then glued to the upper surface of the gratings, see **Fig.9.10**. It was important to remember to check that the grating strips all ran in the same direction, i.e., athwartships when viewed from above.

The edges of the gratings were then trimmed to the outer contours of the 4mm band and then covered with scrap strip. The centre cut-outs were then made and lined and holes drilled for the mounting of the futtock shrouds and deadeyes. It was also convenient at this juncture to drill holes along the front edge of the tops for rigging the crowsfeet as shown in **Fig.9.11**.

Having made all three tops, I then tapered the various mast parts from the dowel provided and constructed the several cross trees and trestle trees, see **Figs 9.12 & 9.13**. The draw-

ings indicate that the lower shrouds be set up before assembling the upper masts. My own preferred method is to assemble the masts complete on the bench before stepping them into the hull. I find this easier in terms of getting everything at the right angle and in line from butt end to truck. On this model, at least, I could see no real disadvantages with either procedure.

## Rigging

The instructions and drawings that showed the sequence and run of the various items of rigging were pretty good, albeit that one has to refer to several sheets and the manual, also familiarise oneself with the identification codes. This is not a criticism of the method used, the writing of such guidelines is an horrendous task and considering the amount of rigging involved, Amati have done quite well.

The most pertinent note in the manual regarding rigging, was the advice to start with the standing rigging, working from bottom to top. For the yards and other running rigging, work from the centre to the outside. This was sound advice and would equally apply to the rigging of most other static models of this type. A further process that many model makers forget or overlook, was to ensure that all of the blocks used were properly drilled. If you happen to miss one, you can be sure that it is always the one that is in the most inaccessible place on the vessel! Remember too, that rings and watch straps are potentially hazardous when getting fingers and hands amongst the rigging.

**Fig. 9.16 The front end, with anchor and buoy rigged to the fore shrouds. Note the clew'd up fore tacks and sheets.**

All standing rigging was set up using black thread.

I think that a word of warning is relevant to the setting up of the lower shrouds. The brass chain plate items that hold the deadeyes in place on the channels were on the soft side and would easily distort if the lanyards between the deadeyes were pulled up too tight.

The futtock shrouds posed another minor problem, in that I had insufficient shaped brass rings for the 5mm deadeyes. Coincidently, the number short was the same number as those I had used for mounting 5mm deadeyes on the main and fore channels. It occurred to me that maybe the latter should have been fixed using ordinary brass wire bent to required shape, but I could find nothing in the English language instructions to that end and, in fact, the 5mm deadeyes are shown only on the Drawing Sheet 1 and are not referred to at all in the instruction manual. However, it was not a disaster and the futtock shrouds were set up using 1mm thread.

The ratlines were added to the shrouds before rigging the back stays which take up quite a bit of finger room. Actually, I left the back stays until the rigging was almost complete for the same reason, they certainly restrict finger access if you put them on earlier.

The various fore and aft stays were then set up to complete the standing rigging as shown in **Fig.9.14 & 9.15**.

The running rigging shown in the manual relates to the model being fitted with sails. If, as in my case, sails were not desired on the model then, obviously, one or two modifications were necessary. The upper yards were lowered to the caps below and the sheets and tacks to the main and fore courses were hauled up by the clue garnets as shown in **Fig.9.16**.

All running rigging was put up using tan coloured thread, see **Figs 9.14 to 9.18**.

The identification of the various bits of rigging, where they went and where they were belayed, was a little time-consuming. For the most part, the drawings and manual seemed reasonably accurate, but I did need to concentrate hard to follow the codes and symbols. However, there appeared to be several notes in the manual which had not been translated into English which led to a little bit of confusion. I would refer particularly to the manual Figs.143, 144, 145 and 151.

Neither drawing nor manual showed braces to the crossjack yard on the mizen mast. A little research indicated that single-block brace pendants hung forward of the crossjack ends and the brace for the starboard pendant started from mid-way up the aft side of the port main shroud. It passed across the vessel, through the pendant block, back to a block on the port shroud and down to the main rail. The brace for the port pendant was similarly rigged across from the starboard main shroud, see **Fig.9.18**.

## Finishing Off

An additional feature that I felt worth considering was main stay tackle used for hoisting boats and hatches, (**Fig.9.17**). Nothing very difficult but something that added that little bit extra.

Coils of rope to hang on the pin rails or lay on the deck as appropriate were made up from the corresponding thicknesses of thread, see **Fig.9.16**. A tedious job this, but one that is essential to complete the model.

A good look around the model revealed several untrimmed,

Fig. 9.17 Amidships, showing the ship's boat and hoisting tackle.

Fig. 9.18　The back end, showing the binnacle between mizen mast and wheel. Note too, the crossjack braces rigged across the vessel via blocks on the shrouds.

or poorly trimmed, ends which needed attention. Odd bits of dust and muck had got into corners and crevices and were blown or brushed out. If you have a camera with a close up lens, you may find it worthwhile scanning the entire model through the viewfinder. The concentrated eye often picks up all sorts of naughties that may otherwise be missed.

## Conclusions

I did find one or two niggling problems. I think that the less experienced modeller might find difficulty jumping about from drawing, to Italian manual, then on to English translation, particularly when it came to the rigging. The omission of the binnacle and the braces to the crossjack yard was somewhat surprising.

However, having said all that, the overall quality and quantity of materials was very good. Castings and etched brass parts simplified the construction of features that modellers often find daunting, i.e., the headrails and stern decoration. The fittings provided were superb and permitted the construction of a very impressive model, but definitely not one for the beginner.

I found the rigging thread extremely good. It took the application of cyanoacrylate very well for sealing knots and permitted the very close trimming of ends. The twist was well-set and didn't open out into several strands when cut.

Value for money? If you want to do a bit of extra research and spend a fair bit of time to build a good Bounty, you won't do much better than this and, at around £175 it is pretty good value.

The kit is distributed by Euro Models, 35 Crown Road, St.Margarets, Twickenham, TW1 3EJ

## References

*"Anatomy of the Ship. The Armed Transport Bounty"* by John McKay Conway ISBN 0 85177 502 0

*"The Masting and Rigging Of English Ships of War 1625 - 1860"* by James Lees Conway ISBN 0 85177 290 0.

# THE AMERICAN WHALING
# BRIG *VIOLA*

My usual brief for Model Boats magazine is to review kits for models of period ships. Being at a time when I was between kits, I thought that it would be a good opportunity to to describe the building of a model that seemed to be a good transitional project between kit and scratch building. There was also the fact that I had a scrap box that was full to overflowing with timber, accumulated over many years of model making. It was also quite some time since I had undertaken a scratch-built model.

There are a number of significant advantages to scratch-building, not the least is the far wider choice of subject matter available. You select your subject, make your own choice of timbers, choose the scale in which you want to work and you do your own research. You can also decide whether you are going to make a purely visual replica of the subject vessel, or try to reproduce the actual constructional techniques involved. Thus, at the end of the day, whether the model stands or falls is entirely dependent on your craftsmanship, not the least of which is your ability to improvise should your facilities be less than you would like.

With regard to cost, much depends upon the sort of workshop equipment that you have available and whether or not you have to purchase pre-sized strip wood and perhaps some commercial fittings. Some sort of lathe, even if it is only one of the very small 12 volt units, is almost an essential and will enable you to make quite a number of turned parts that you would otherwise have to buy from your model shop. Generally speaking, except maybe for the smaller models, I have not found too much difference in cost between kit and scratch-building. Obviously, the farther you progress into model making, the cheaper it becomes, because you accumulate timber, and you make jigs and special tools that can be used over and over again.

Research can be quite a pricey item in your agenda, particularly if travel is involved to any great extent. Drawings are not cheap, specialist books are not often available through your local library on loan, and postal enquiries are long-winded. If you do use the mail, please remember to enclose return postage, particularly if addressing an overseas source. The Internet can be very helpful once you have identified suitable sources and sites. However, I don't think you should rush out to buy a computer solely for research into model boats!

Having made these very general comments, the Viola seemed to me to be the ideal project to introduce scratch-building to the model maker who had hitherto only dealt with kits. The lines were relatively simple, the brigantine rig not too complex and the deck fittings perhaps sufficiently different, being a whaler, to present an interesting challenge. Assuming that many modellers reading this article will have had a number of kit built models under their belts, I have referred to kit building techniques where appropriate. Where features are perhaps a little more unusual, I have gone into greater detail concerning the methods and procedures I adopted.

## Research

My choice of subject was inspired mainly by an interest in the American whaling industry. I was fortunate, in that I had made a number of visits to the eastern side of the U.S.A. and had had many opportunities to visit places like Mystic Seaport, New Bedford, etc. The wealth of material on the subject of whaling in those parts is quite staggering, much of it available by post or via the Internet. It was from a list of ship plans by Walter Channing that I selected the drawings for Viola.

Of course, the real art of research is knowing the right questions to ask and, for example, in the case of Viola, there were two typical items, amongst others, which could have been overlooked. The design of the American flag in 1910 and the use of the abbreviation ME for Maine on the transom, neither being obvious areas where the model maker may go astray. One thing that can be relied on though, is that somewhere out there, is someone who will not only spot your errors but also be very quick to let you know.

The plans came on two sheets at a scale of 1/64 although I chose to increase the scale of my model to 1/48. I thought that there would not be too much further research to do, since the detail given was quite comprehensive, but it was surprising just how many questions cropped up during the course of the building process.

Viola was built in Essex, Massachusetts in 1910 and, according to Channing's drawings, registered in Portland, Maine, although I understand that she worked mostly out of New Bedford for the brief seven years of her life. She completed four voyages into the Atlantic, but was lost with all hands on her fifth voyage in 1917.

The vessel was an hermaphrodite brig and during her first voyage was reckoned to be oversparred. Thus, yards were shortened and sails modified, Walter Channing's drawings showing both the original and modified set-ups. She was of timber construction, having a length of 125ft and a beam of 26ft with a displacement of 190 tons.

Four boats were carried, two on davits to port, one on davits to starboard and one on bearers across the stern. The boats were of traditional design, that is, double-ended in order to facilitate a "Stern All" command to quickly pull back from a troublesome whale. The construction of the boats is, in itself, a challenge for the model maker.

The other main feature of the vessel was, of course, the tryworks, where pieces of the whale were rendered down to oil. The tryworks were essentially two integral ovens below huge iron open-topped bowls. The fire was contained by a fire brick carcase inside a three-sided iron casing.

The whale, having been caught was hauled up, head uppermost, on the starboard side of the ship through the cutting stage. The head was first emptied of spermaceti, then the remainder of the carcase cut into blankets of blubber and taken below where it was further reduced to "horse pieces" ready for trying out or boiling in the tryworks iron pots. The oil was then bailed into a cooling tank at the side of the tryworks from where it was put into barrels. Trying out could be a day and night job, bearing in mind that an average sized sperm whale yielded about 50 barrels of oil. In his book, "The Charles W. Morgan," John F. Leavitt paints a very descriptive picture of the crew working at night. "The smoke and occasional flare-up of flames provided a lurid scene, particularly at night when the crew, working in the dim light of a few lanterns, looked like characters from Dante's Inferno."

## Selecting Materials

Starting totally from scratch is, perhaps, a little more simple than having to work around that material you may already have. As I mentioned earlier, my model would be constructed on the same basis as a kit, therefore I needed plywood or basswood (European lime) for the false keel. Bearing in mind the size of the model at a scale of 1/48, a minimum of 6mm thickness was fairly essential for stability and strength. The frames could also be cut from the same material athough basswood or lime would make it easier when it came to doing the edge work necessary to provide adequate seating for the planking.

Deck planking was made in two widths, the exposed fore and aft decks using 4mm wide strips, and the working area amidships sheathed with planks double that width.

For the hull planking, I chose 5 x 2mm lime for the upper sheathing and 4 x 1mm for the lower. Since the hull would be painted, I selected lime for all planking. However, if you wished to leave the hull in natural wood finish, a second planking of, say, 4 x 1mm walnut or mahogany would be a reasonable choice. Remember that the lower parts of the vessel were copper-plated and this had to be given some thought. I decided that I would make some tiles of 1.0mm thick strip and fit each piece individually. A long task, but the effect is somewhat better than just painting a plain surface with copper-coloured paint.

I chose to make the yards from dowel rod I already had in my scrap box, but the masts, I decided to turn down from some nice square-section pieces of ramin.

For the various fittings, much would depend on the facilities and skills you have available, as to whether you make or buy. In actual fact, apart from blocks, deadeyes and rudder hinges, most of the bits required for Viola are probably not available commercially anyway.

Deck cabins, companionways, skylight and bins were made from a combination of ply, wood strip and plasticard. Nothing obligatory here, I use the medium I have to hand or with which I can work best. If it gives the result I want, I'll use it!

With regard to paints, black, white grey and gold were used on the original vessel. The decks were natural wood which, for the model, I would use matt or satin varnish. The bare wood surfaces of the hull would certainly benefit from a coat of grey primer before painting.

## Adhesives

Maybe a word or two about adhesives would be in order. Most modellers, I guess, have their favourite brands but, in general terms, white PVA for wood, a two-part epoxy for the wood to metal jobs, cyanoacrylate for the very small bits and knot sealing, plus Plastic Weld for any plasticard work, will fit the bill.

There are rumblings in some quarters about the efficacy of some adhesives in the long term. I have used all of the above stickies for many, many years and, as far as I am aware, no model of mine has yet fallen apart. However, I have always

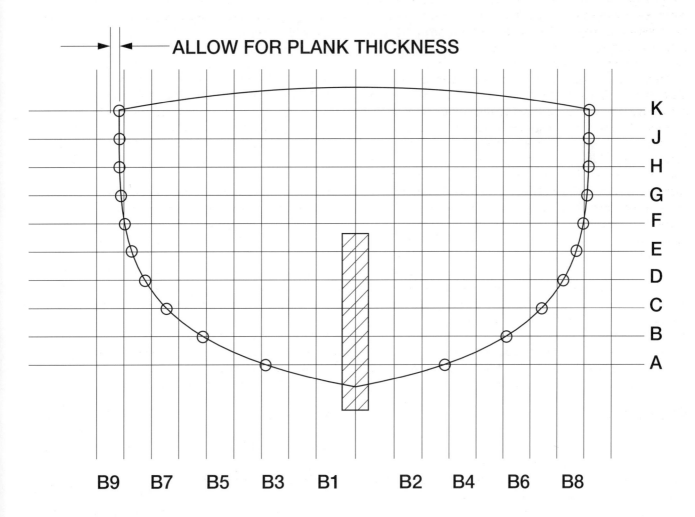

**Fig. 10.1 Layout of frames.**

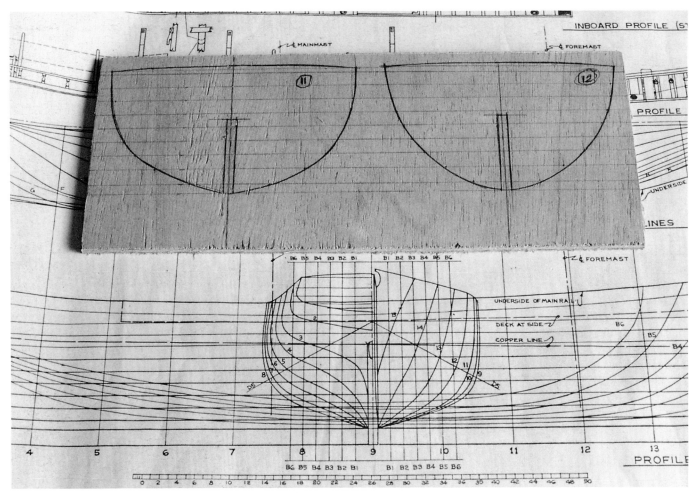

Fig. 10.2  Two frames drawn directly on to the wood.

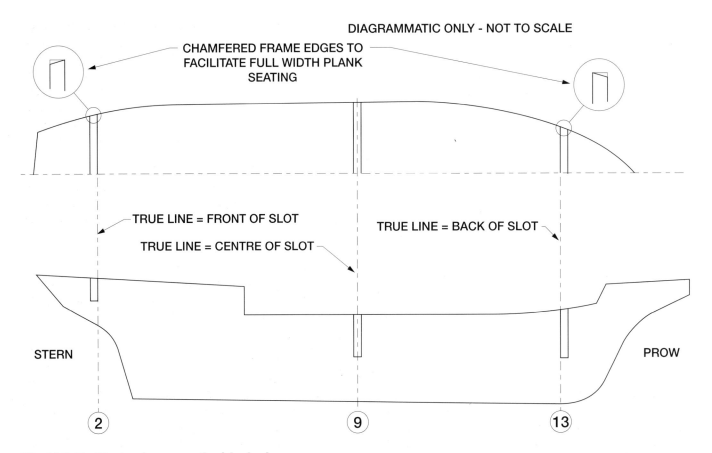

Fig. 10.3  Positioning frames on the false keel.

**Fig. 10.4 Hull carcass being deck planked.**

observed three golden rules. Use the right adhesive for the material in hand, use it in accordance with the manufacturer's recommendations and, where possible, make a sound mechanical joint in addition to using the glue. A typical example of the latter would be bitts and pin rails, which should be dowelled to the deck rather than relying on merely a glued butt joint.

A note of caution about knot sealing with cyano. Don't put the nozzle of the bottle on the knot and squeeze, use a toothpick type applicator. The knot does not need to be soaked in adhesive, in fact, if the glue penetrates right through the thread it will become brittle and can break. This may be one of the sources of the rumblings concerning long-term degrading, as might long-term exposure to high humidity or damp conditions.

## Marking Out

The first task to be faced is the transferring of shapes from plans to timber, specifically the false keel and frames. This involves the accurate measurement of the ship's lines on the plan and reproducing them either on to paper or directly on to the wood being used.

If you have the use of a computer with a scanner or some sort of draughting program available, the frames can be individually reproduced and printed out on A4 sheets. The false keel would need to be plotted on to several sheets, transferring a common line or feature, sheet to sheet for correct alignment

purposes. Any alteration to scale should be readily accomplished with the software. Each item would then have to be carefully cut out and pasted to the selected timber.

The second method would be similar to the first, but manually drawing each feature on to paper. This is what many would call the "Fun Method" and calls for a degree of draughtsmanship and geometry. Alternatively, if you have to use this drawing method, then you can draw directly on to the face of your timber.

A quicker and more accurate method, particularly if you are altering scale as I was, is to use the services of a photocopier. The trick here is to plan exactly what you want before the operator starts pressing buttons: the cost can quickly mount up even at a few pence per sheet!

If you choose to follow either of the manual methods, there are some factors that are essential to doing a good job. As mentioned earlier, accuracy and symmetry are of paramount importance. A chisel-pointed 3H pencil will give a sharp line without too much resharpening. A square, a long straight-edge, a fairly large pair of compasses and dividers, a good finely-graduated scale rule and, if possible, a set of French or ship's curves will provide the fairly essential drawing kit. If you are altering the scale of the original plans, proportional dividers would prove an invaluable asset.

The lines given on the plans normally define the outer surface of the hull so, therefore, the shape that you draw has to be the plank thickness inside the given shape, see **Fig.10.1**. Don't forget to mark the number of the frame inside the line

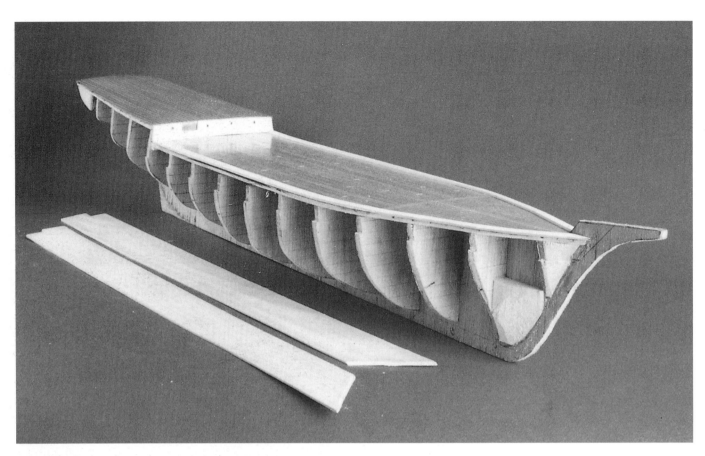

Fig. 10.5  The carcass with waterways and fascia in place. Initially shaped bulwarks ready for assembly into 2mm recesses in frames

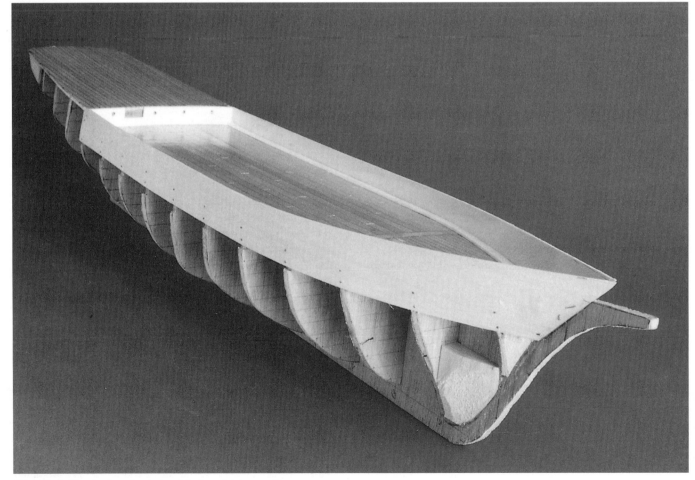

Fig. 10.6  The bulwarks assembled and trimmed.

**Fig. 10.7 The planked basic hull.**

of the profile, that way the identification always stays with the piece. The "drawn on wood" result is shown in **Fig.10.2**.

Remember, too, that the position of each frame shape is given at one precise position or plane along the length of the keel. Thus, when determining the position of the cross-halving slots for frame-to-keel fitting, the back of the slot will be on true position on frames toward the front of the hull, the front of the slot will be on true position on frames toward the stern, and the slot will be equally spaced about the true position on frames amidships. This is so that when you later trim and chamfer the edges of the frames to provide a full width seating for the planking you maintain true sectional lines at the correct positions along the keel, see **Fig.10.3**. I made the top lines of the false keel to coincide with the level of the two main decks. The depth of the cross-halving slots was such that the tops of the frames corresponded to the top of the false keel.

Depending on how smooth the surface is of your chosen timber for the frames and false keel, you may find it helpful to apply a coat of primer before you start drawing. This helps the drawn lines to show up more clearly when using the fret or band saw later on.

## Building the Hull Carcase

One of the major differences that you have to face when scratch-building, as against kit construction, is the fact that you have no instructions. If you have made up a few kits, you probably won't have any worries about how to do things, but you will have to take care as to the sequence of putting things together. This means a lengthy study of the drawings and the making of notes.

On the Viola, the line of the bulwarks rail is coincident with the waterway of the poop deck, aft. I therefore decided to first

assemble the frames to the false keel then, to stabilise this structure, put on false decks. This also helps to give support when you bevel the edges of the frames, which was the next job listed.

To keep things simpler, I decided that I would plank the deck next, before making the basic bulwark construction, see **Fig.10.4**. This meant that I had total access to the whole deck area for scraping, sanding and finishing. The wood selected for the deck planking was checked for identical thickness and each edge blackened with a chisel-pointed marker pen to represent the caulking.

The edges of each of the relevant frames were then recessed to a position about 12mm below deck level and to a depth of 2mm to provide a location and seating for the bulwark pieces to be added later. The decks were then planked, noting that the central working area was sheathed with a greater width of planking to that laid on the forecastle and after decks. These planks were laid down on top of the conventional decking beneath, in order that they may be more readily lifted and replaced at sea when the ravages of work dictated. The edges of the deck planking were trimmed to suit the tops of the frames at the stern and the bulwark slots cut in those frames amidships to prow.

This trimmed line was then used to determine the outer edge of the waterway for the main deck. I simply laid a suitable thickness of sheet timber on to the planked deck and marked the shape with a pencil. Having cut the sheet to this line, I drew a parallel line to determine the width of the waterway. This was then well-sanded and painted before assembly. The essential task here was to get the finished width parallel throughout its length without any lumps and bumps - not difficult, just needed a bit of care.

The fascia for the stern cabin was put in place before fitting the bulwarks. These were made from 2mm basswood cut

Fig. 10.8 "Copper plating" in progress.

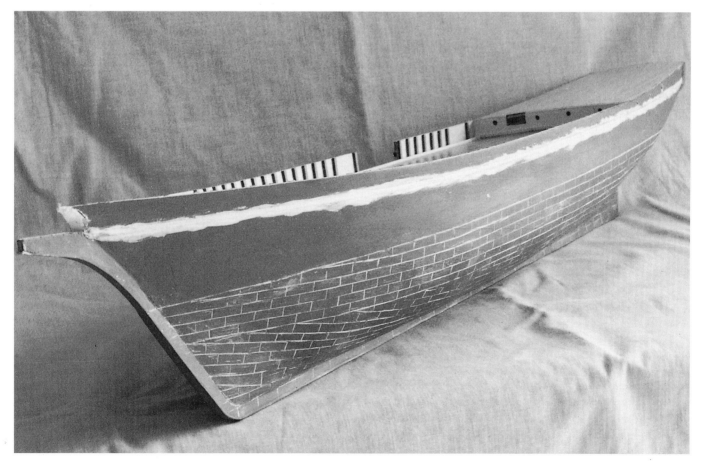

Fig. 10.9 The plated bottom primed and grouted.

**Fig. 10.10 Railing pieces at the prow.**

initially well oversize at their top edge. When fitted into the recesses previously cut into the tops of the frames, then pinned and glued, they were flush with, and followed the lines of the hull to perfection. Taking a fair number of check dimensions from the drawings, the top edge of the bulwarks were marked and cut to size, see **Fig.10.6**.

## Hull Planking

There were three specific areas of planking to be considered. The top portion of the bulwarks was to be planked with 1mm planking, below that to the copper line with 2mm material, and the coppered area itself which I had decided to "tile" with individual pieces. I first put in position the 2 x 2mm beading along the bulwarks that marked the line between the two different thickness of planking in that area. This strip was ultimately to be painted white so, to make life easier later on, I very lightly took the sharp edges off the timber and gave it a coat of white paint before assembly. Removing the edges will help guide the brush later on when painting the final white lining.

The 1mm planking was then laid above the beading to the top of the bulwarks. This thinner timber provides a recess along the hull into which the chain plates will later be fixed.

The 2mm main planking below the beading down to the copper line was put in place with pins and glue. The pins were removed after the glue had cured and the whole surface rubbed down before applying a coat of sanding sealer. After a final rub down, the transom plate was put in place and the

whole hull given a coat of grey primer. This highlighted any dents, bumps, or other imperfections that needed attention before moving on to the coppered area.

The base surface for the coppered area was planked with 1mm material in the conventional manner, the pins removed and the wood rubbed down to produce an even surface upon which to lay the "copper" tiles. The planked hull is shown in Fig.10.7. Further research, and with the help of The Kendall Whaling Museum, I established probable sizes for the plates and that mine could reasonably made from 6 x 1mm strip. I was pretty sure that it was still possible to buy copper plating complete with embossed fixing heads, but I also remembered that when I had seen them, I had felt that they looked very artificial.

It was important to make all the plates the same length and the easiest way to do this is to make a simple jig. I bevelled the two long edges of one face of the strip before cutting the individual plates. This was done to ensure that the lines of the plates were prominent after assembly. Thus, before I glued each piece in place, I also had to bevel the two short edges. The size of the bevel was about half the thickness of the strip, so that after final sanding down, some of the delineating bevel still remained, see **Fig.10.8**. A slight bend needed to be induced into some of the plates where the hull curves were more acute. This was easily accomplished with a plank nipper.

Having got all of the plates on the lower part of the hull, I gave the whole area a coat of primer. Then, using Model Lite filler, I grouted between the plates. This was applied with the finger, the pad of which impressed itself to just the right

Fig. 10.11 The finished rails at the prow.

Fig. 10.12 Making the slots for the chain plates.

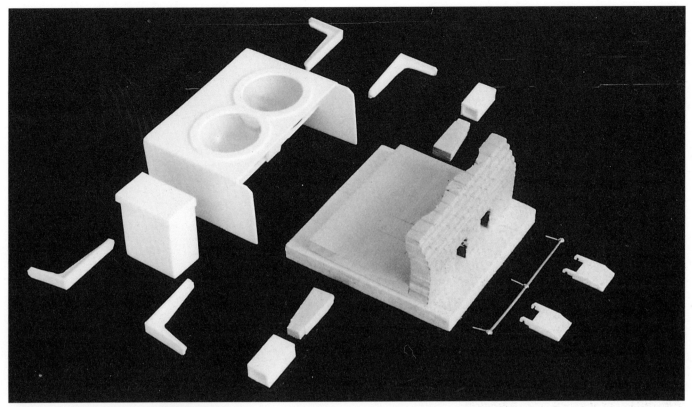

**Fig. 10.13 The try works components.**

**Fig. 10.14 The assembled try works.**

depth. I didn't want to finish up with too sharp an outline around each plate, just a subtle hint that the surface was in fact plated. A couple of thin coats of paint later on would finish the hull off as required. The plated surface at this stage is shown in **Fig.10.9**.

The stanchions on the inner faces of the bulwarks were then put in place, again see **Fig.10.9**. Very careful measurement and the making of a simple width gauge ensured that the stanchions were equally spaced along the length of the bulwarks. The reinforcements for the several hawse holes were also put in place at this juncture, the inner and outer embellishments

for these holes being oval rings made from 2mm diameter brass wire with soldered butt joints.

All these inner surfaces had to be painted white and I considered that it would be easier to do this in two stages. I immediately painted everywhere except the outer faces of the stanchions. The lashing rails were then glued in place, then these were painted together with the stanchion outer faces. This procedure helped to avoid excess paint accumulating at the joints between stanchions and rails. It also helped to ensure that everywhere did indeed get painted!

## The Bulwark Rails

The rails were in fact a continuation of the waterways to the decks at prow and stern and, being all on the one level, were thus treated as one project. I cut all parts from 2mm thick basswood.

I first made the pieces that went across the vessel at the stern, the front of the poop deck and the rear of the forecastle deck. The shaped prow piece was also made at this time, see Fig.10.10. I chose this procedure so that each of these parts could more simply include the corner fillets where necessary. All internal edges were painted before assembly. The longitudinal shape of each item was traced from the actual outline at the top of the hull and the inside line of the rail carefully drawn to be parallel to it. The outer edge was left full for final shaping after assembly to provide the best possible match between all of the separate pieces, see **Fig.10.11**.

Recesses were cut in the areas where the chain plates were to be assembled. A notched strip was then fitted into each recess, thus leaving a series of rectangular slots for the chain plates to pass through the rail, see **Fig.10.12**. The strip was then trimmed to match the outer edge of the rail. This was considered both easier and safer than trying to cut slots through the finished rail.

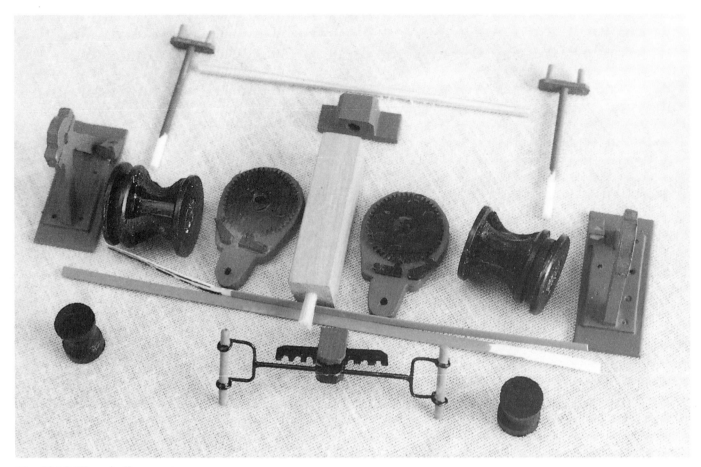

Fig. 10.15 The windlass parts.

Fig. 10.16 Deck fittings forward.

**Fig. 10.17 Deck fittings 'midships.**

The name, Viola, appears in the conventional position on the bows, port and starboard. It is also displayed across the upper area of the transom, below which is the port of registration, Portland, Maine. These were in raised lettering and I chose to use Slater's Plastikard letters of suitable size. However, doubts had been raised as to whether the name, Maine, should be used or, as Channing's drawings depicted, the abbreviation, ME. The archives at The Kendall Whaling Museum, revealed old photographs which showed that Channing was correct and I am indebted to them for their invaluable help in this and several other matters concerning the Viola.

## The Try Works

This is the feature around which the whole on-board operation revolved. It basically comprised two iron pots, housed above a dual oven facility in fire brick, that exhausted into two chimneys. The ovens and pots were encased in iron on three sides and top, the front was exposed firebrick with four or five of the top courses stepped back. In order to protect the deck below, the try works assembly was mounted on what was essentially a shallow tank of water, called a goose pen.

I used 2mm thick lime strips, suitably notched to represent the fire bricks and assembled them to a wooden base as the core of my try works unit. The pots were made from a plastic ball cut into two hemispheres and the main casing made up from 1mm Plasticard. This material was also used to fabricate the four angle brackets that fix the try works to the deck and to make the cooling tank that stood alongside. The various bits and pieces are featured in **Fig.10.13**.

There was nothing too difficult in this part of the project, the main point to watch being the seating of the unit on the cambered deck. The angle brackets thus had to have an included angle slightly beyond ninety degrees to suit. The complete assembly is shown in **Fig.10.14**.

## The Windlass

This feature was probably the most demanding of all the deck fittings to make. A central samson post supported a bearing for the main shaft on its aft face, and a bracket to house the rocker assembly on the front. Each side of the samson post was a pawl and ratchet unit operated by the rocker assembly. The main windlass drums and braking devices were outboard of the ratchets and the extreme ends of the shaft were supported by an "A" frame. These parts are shown in **Fig.10.15**.

The windlass construction illustrated totally the difference between scratch and kit building. Making each of the sub-assemblies was straightforward enough needing, perhaps, a little innovative imagination to select materials. The real key to success in the total construction was to realise that all the various bits had to be finally put together in situ on deck. This was because the main shaft alignment had to be though the two "A" frames and the central bearing on the samson post, at the same time taking into account the camber of the deck. The height of the rocker assembly on the fore face of the post had to recognise the linking positions on the ends of the ratchet units. The brake bands were made from plasticard strip as were the tightening rods and handles, again assembly taking place after the "A" frames and main shaft had been fixed in position.

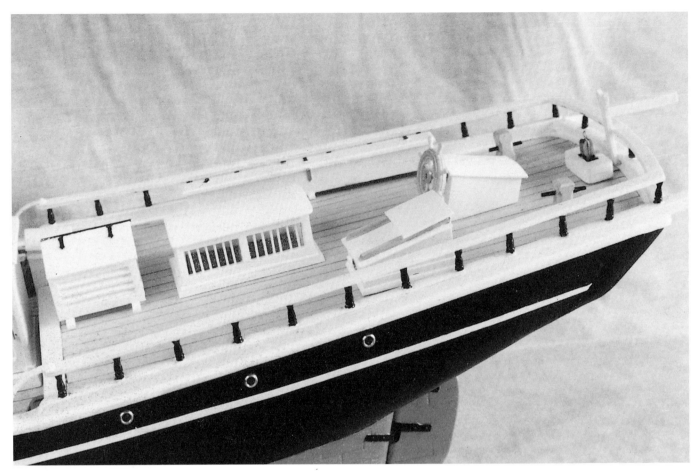

Fig. 10.18  Deck fittings aft.

Fig. 10.19  A simple pin jig to help make the davits.

**Fig. 10.20 The davits, cranes and crane supports.**

All these procedures would normally be the subject of a kit instruction manual, here, as a scratch builder, you need to apply foresight to work things out for yourself.

## Deck Fittings

The deck fittings, hatches, companionways, bins and boxes were make from pieces of thin ply or, in the case of the panelled doors, Plasticard sheet. The inner and outer rims to the hawse holes were made from 2mm dia. brass wire soldered into suitably-sized oval rings.

Fife rails, bitts and bollards were all dowelled and glued to the deck for added strength. Like the windlass, the fife rails comprised a winding shaft controlled by two pawl and ratchet assemblies, port and starboard. Within the confines of the fife rails were the two diaphragm type pumps. The deck fittings are shown in position in **Figs.10.16, 10.17 and 10.18**.

The davits and boat cranes were made from suitably-sized strip wood. It was found that it was worth a little bit of extra time to knock up a couple of jigs to ensure that the six boat cranes were all identical and that the angles on the davits were the same. Nothing too sophisticated was needed, just a few pins at strategic places driven into a piece of scrap ply, see Figs.19 and 20. The boat cranes are hinged to vertical bearers which act as rubbing strips when the boats are raised and lowered. These items were not assembled to the hull until much later in the building process.

## The Stand

Having made the hull and the deck fittings, it was time to make the stand. Up until this stage I had used a cradle from a long-gone model as a temporary support but, before assembling everything on to the deck, and certainly before thinking about masts and spars, a firm, square and true base was essential. The message here is not to spoil the ship with any old rough piece of timber that happens to be the right size. Have a search around the wood yards for something a bit special.

There are several designs that can be adopted for a stand, it is really a matter of personal preference. I chose the base and pedestal style purely because it suited the environment into which the model was to be exhibited, but the cradle design would have been just as practical.

## The Bowsprit

The bowsprit had three tapers. The longest taper, from the prow forward, blends into a short tapered section at the tip. A band with four shackles was placed at the juncture of these two tapers. The third, reverse taper, is on that part of the bowsprit inboard, running under the forecastle deck to butt against the windlass samson post. A further band and shackle was positioned at the prow for the forestay and eyebolts positioned for the fore topmast stay and the inner bobstay rigging. **Fig.10.21** refers.

Wood jackstays were also fitted on the upper port and starboard quarters of the bowsprit, these being fashioned from 3 x 1mm box wood. Cut-outs were filed along one edge of the strip, taking care to space them evenly. The strips were then glued to the bowsprit and, when completely set, the plain edge was lightly planed to leave a width of about 2mm.

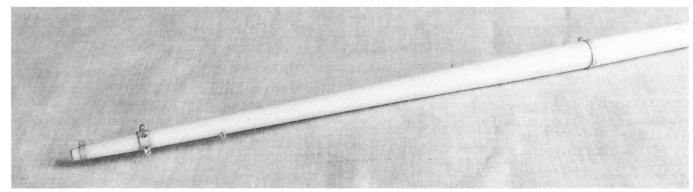

Fig. 10.21  The bowsprit and bands.

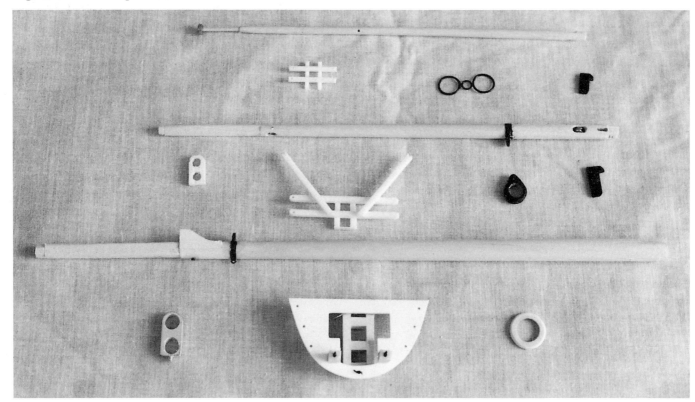

Fig. 10.22  The foremast parts.

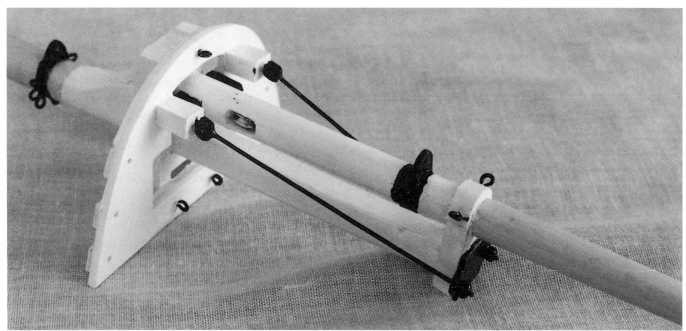

Fig. 10.23  The fore top.

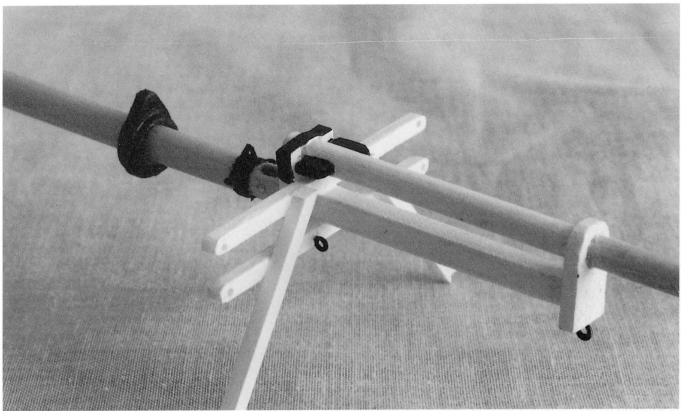

Fig. 10.24  The fore topmast cross trees.

## The Masts and Spars

The construction of the masts was not something to be started without thought. There are four yards on the foremast and two booms on the main. The attachment of these items to their respective masts called for considerable detailed work, some of which needed to be considered before making and assembling the major parts. Spiderband, top, caps, crosstrees, the upper topsail yard tub and mast rings had to be assembled in the correct order otherwise you could finish up with a bit over and no way to put it in place!

Concentrating on the foremast first, I made the three primary poles from some square-sectioned ramin that had been lurking around in my scrap box for a number of years. These were first squared and octagoned on the taper, spun in my small 12 volt lathe to finished sizes. Slots were then drilled and filed in position to take the fids. The supports for the fore yard truss and lower topsail yard were then put in place.

The construction of the fore top, cross-trees and caps really needs no explanation except to say that it was highly desirable to check what holes and eyebolts were going to be needed before assembling them to the mast parts. It should also be remembered that the topsail yard is attached to the mast by a sliding tub which must be slid onto the mast before assembling cross-trees. All of the foremast parts can be seen in **Fig.10.22**. and the assembled tops in **Figs.10.23, 10.24 and 10.25**.

The notes above for the foremast also apply, of course, to the main mast. Additionally, there are bands around the upper part of the lower mast to which the peak halliard blocks are attached, see **Fig.10.26**. Also, there are rings around the mast to which sails are attached, whether or not sails are actually going to be hung. A further small point about the rings, if you use standard brass rings, solder the butt joints and paint them before assembly.

It was important to accurately position on the main mast the ring that supports the jaws of the main-sail boom. When sitting on the boom crotch, the boom should be basically horizontal and its underside be clear of the top of the galley. Sufficient space should be allowed for rigging the boom retaining tackle.

The four yards on the foremast were tapered in the usual fashion and slots put in the ends of the three lower spars to house pulleys. Jackstays were fitted to all yards in the same manner as for the bowsprit. The trusses can be made from suitably thick timber, preferably box or pear wood or, even Plasticard, if the more exotic timbers are hard to come by. Whatever material is used the main consideration was to provide a strong joint between truss and yard. The top gallant yard is held to the mast by a wooden saddle and parrals. The footropes, fitted to all four yards, were made from florists' coated wire. This is cheating a bit but, at scales usually adopted by model makers, the normal threads available seem to have a mind of their own and just don't hang right, see **Fig.10.27**.

The boom and gaff on the main mast are simple enough poles but it was noted that on the gaff, the jaws were fitted with a tilting shoe. This adjusts itself to the face of the mast no matter what angle the gaff is rigged relative to the mast. Such a device was not apparently fitted to the boom since this spar was always in the near horizontal position.

The masts were then stepped, taking care to recognise the correct lean. Spars and yards were not assembled at this time since they would impede hand and finger space during the putting up of the standing rigging.

## The Whaleboats

I have seen several models of whalers without boats and, of course, there were times when such status prevailed. However,

**Fig. 10.25 The foremast head rings**

**Fig. 10.26 The mainmast top.**

I decided that the overall effect of the model would be enhanced if the boats were depicted on their respective davits and bearers.

These boats were a major project in themselves. Channing's drawings showed enough to suggest that they were of a design developed by James Beetle, i.e., batten-seam construction. This involved eight planks each side of the boat. The garboard plank, that adjacent to the keel, was lapped by the edge of the lowest of five carvel planks with the two planks below the gunwales being lapstraked. The seams between the five carvel planks were battened on the inside. Thus the basic description was 3 laps, 4 battens, 8 planks.

The problems I faced were two-fold. First, how much detail to try and reproduce, and second, how best to make four identical boats.

There was a host of gear kept in each boat from line tubs, harpoons, lances and oars, through to mast and sail. Line tubs contained the tow-lines that were attached to the irons first used on the whale. The larger tub generally housed 225 fathoms of line coiled down and the smaller tub, 75 fathoms.

The first two "live" harpoons or irons, would normally be carried resting in the bow chocks and boat crotch ready for action, although it is doubtful whether this was the case with the boats on davits. Some boats may have even carried a Pierce and Eggar's shoulder gun for bomb lances. The mast, with sail lashed to it, laid in the boat along with the oars.

The oars used in an American whaleboat were the longest in general use. The five pulling oars could be anything from 14ft to 18ft and the steering oar as much as 25ft in length, depending upon the design and style of the boat. The blade of each oar was marked with identifying bands to ensure its use in the correct position, the different lengths used to compensate for the severe curvature of the boat's sides. Rowing was

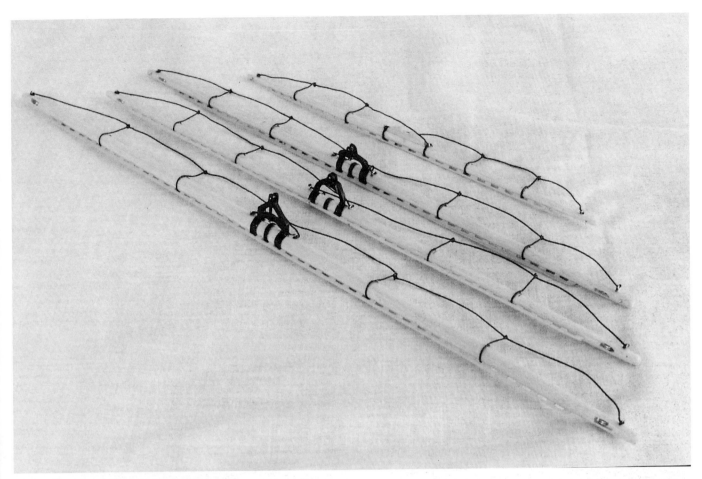

Fig. 10.27 The yards. Note the jackstays.

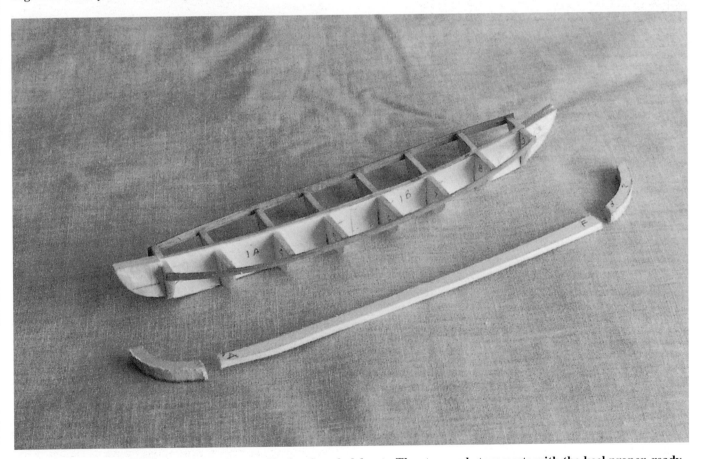

Fig. 10.28 The false keel and bulkhead assembly for the whaleboats. The stem and stern posts with the keel proper, ready to be dry pinned in place.

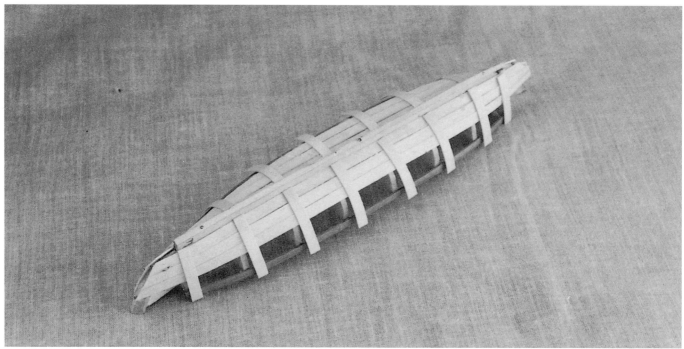

**Fig. 10.29  The inner ceiling and major ribs in place.**

done across the boat, that is, the oarsman would sit on the opposite side of the boat to which his relative rowlock was located, thus affording greater leverage.

So, how much of this lot to put in? The answer has to lie in the limitations of the modeller and his equipment and the depth of his research. It was felt that it was best not to try to portray everything, but get right what was attempted. I thus decided to leave three boats as basic shells with just rudder slung on the stern port side. On the fourth, on the starboard davits, I would include a more representative set of equipment.

The second problem that I faced was how best to make four identical boats and, at the same time, comply as closely as possible with the specifications of design. Each boat was to finish up at 7.3" long which, of course, meant a considerable amount of internal detail. Having studied the full size design and construction, I reckoned that it would be best to build my boats on a removable core structure, thus ensuring that each boat would be basically the same. Thus, I made a false keel and bulkhead assembly (**Fig.10.28**), to follow the inside lines of the boat and first positioned keel, prow and stern-post, pinning each to the core structure. I then planked in the ceiling part-way up the hull from the keel, applying glue only to the end posts and to each other. The edges of the core frames had previously been waxed to ensure that I didn't accidently glue the core in place! I bent and laid in ribs on the outside surface of the ceiling planks (**Fig.10.29**). I then put on the outer planking, remembering that the garboard strake was lapped.

When all adhesive had thoroughly cured, I removed the pins from keel and posts in order to remove the core, see **Fig.10.30**, ready to start again.

The completion of each boat was carried out as a group of four in order to better attain an identical result. This involved adding the fore and aft standing platforms, logger head, lion's tongue and thwarts, as shown in **Fig.10.31**.

Apart from the platforms which were sawn timber, the inside of the boat was painted grey. The outside surfaces were

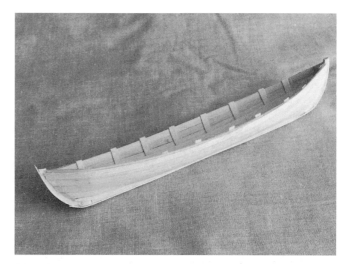

**Fig. 10.30  The outer planking done and the false core removed**

white with the lapstraked planks at the gunwales, black. The four completed boats are shown in **Fig.10.32**.

## Standing Rigging

All standing rigging was set up using black thread, including the ratlines and shroud lanyards. All thread was treated with white PVA adhesive to lay down surface hairs and to give an added degree of stiffness to the material. I applied the glue to the pads of forefinger and thumb, then pulled the cut length of thread through several times. Each pull distributed the glue increasingly evenly over the length of thread. Pressure between finger and thumb applied tension to the thread and took much of the natural twist out of the material. This is particularly beneficial when tightening up standing rigging and largely avoids deadeyes twisting out of line as the line is tensioned. Alternatively, thread can be hanked up, washed and stretched with weights while drying, but I have found that the

**Fig. 10.31  Internal fitting out.**

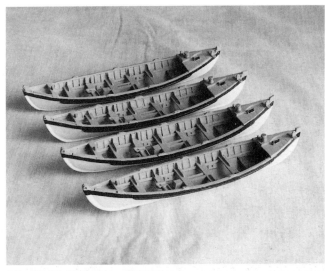

**Fig. 10.32  Four completed boats.**

PVA treatment gives a more stable result.

The lower and upper shrouds were put up first, together with their ratlines. Tying ratlines is something of a tedious task, but can be made easier by applying them immediately after setting up the shrouds. Without the backstays in place there was much more finger room in which to manipulate tweezers and tie all the knots. A piece of plain, light-coloured card, (avoiding white), or paper behind the shrouds provided a good background for working and certainly made things easier on the eyes.

I would caution against trying to maintain correct spacing of the ratlines by eye. The brain can be easily deceived by the converging verticals of the shrouds and the constant variation of shape enclosed by shrouds and ratlines as you progress up from deck level to mast head. A strip of card cut to desired width, or a pair of dividers will help to keep things under control.

The bowsprit shrouds and bobstays were rigged next, followed by the fore and aft stays to the fore and main masts. The backstays to both masts were the last of the standing rigging to be put up, enabling a balance of tension to the whole system to be attained.

Copies of early photographs of Viola clearly show safety netting below the bowsprit. A visit to the local haberdasher's proved fruitful and I was able to purchase a small piece of black net material used for dressmaking. This was lashed to the bowsprit shrouds then trimmed to shape, see **Fig.10.33**.

I also chose to rig the anchors at this stage. The chain lock-er was well back amidships and it was easier to run the chain before I got too much rigging in the way.

## The Running Rigging

Tan-coloured thread was used throughout, but again given the PVA treatment as before.

It was decision time again! Feature sails in full rig, show them furled on the yards, or hide them away in the sail lockers below? Since I have not yet discovered a material that completely meets all the requirements for scale sails in terms of weave, area to weight ratio and that elusive "hanging right" quality, I chose the third option. This would mean that the yards would be lowered down to the caps and the gaff would be lowered to a position parallel to, and almost resting on the boom. The boom itself would be dropped on to the boom crotch aft. It also had to be remembered that the position of many blocks would have to be adjusted accordingly.

There were few belaying points indicated on the drawings, so further research was necessary. Fortunately, much of the rigging is a matter of common sense and, once it is understood what each line does, its path through the masts and spars becomes reasonably apparent. None the more for that, it was found advisable not to permanently tie off at pin rails until all the rigging had been put up, when it could be seen that all lines had a free run. This makes final belaying a little more fiddly, I agree, but I found it to be worth the extra care. A good tip for temporary belaying is to thread the fall of the tackle

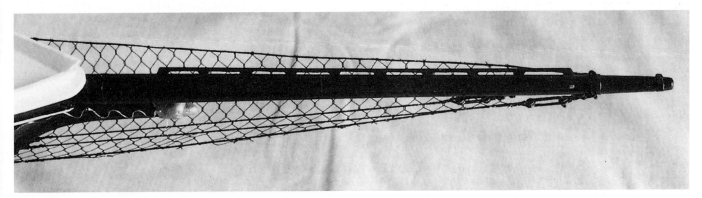

**Fig. 10.33  The bowsprit netting.**

Fig. 10.34 Rigging to the mainmast. Note the three blocks for the peak halliards.

Fig. 10.35 Anchors rigged. The stays'l downhauls are tied off to cleats on the foredeck.

concerned down through the pin rail and wedge it in place with the tip of a belaying pin. At the end of the rigging process each line and pin was removed one at a time, the pin replaced and the proper lashing made.

Again, a bit of forward planning paid dividends. I tried to proceed in such a way that, at all times, I had the optimum amount of finger space to thread rigging and to tie off knots and lashings. In general terms, it is easier to work from deck level, upwards and from the centre line of the hull, outwards, but leaving the braces until the very last, since being able to swivel them out of the way was a distinct advantage. In fact, on this model I left them until after I had set up the boats on their respective davits. Blocks were rigged to masts and spars, as far as possible, before assembly.

In general terms, ropes and blocks became smaller and lighter as the rigging rose from deck, aloft. There is fairly well-documented records of these sizes for naval vessels, but details are much harder, if not impossible, to find for the smaller commercial vessel. However, it would be wrong of the modeller to ignore the situation and sensible sizes of threads should be selected accordingly.

The Boom. The jaws of the boom are held against the main mast by tackle along the underside of the boom. The main sheet rigging down to the buffer block was pulled up taut to keep the boom stable in the boom crotch.

The Gaff. Rigged with three peak halliard single sheave blocks on its upper side. The double running halliard was rove through three blocks on the aft side of the mast, the centre one being a two sheave block, see **Fig.10.34**. The throat halliard

was set up using a pair of three sheave blocks. A lashing around the boom and gaff kept everything in place and permitted the rigging to be better applied.

The Stays'l Rig. Halliards and downhauls to main and foremasts were set up on the underside of their respective stays. For the stays'ls to the foremast, the halliards were belayed at the spider band and the downhauls to cleats on the fore-deck. For those to the foremast, the halliards were tied off at the main fife rail and the downhauls to the foremast spider band.

The Yards. Lifts, halliards and clews were rigged to all yards basically in that order before adding the sheets and other tackle, see **Fig.10.36**. This gave some progressive stability to the set-up and, for the same reason, what was done on the starboard side was immediately balanced by the same procedure on the port side. When all of the yards had been temporarily belayed and correct tensions throughout had been shown to be attainable, each rope was permanently belayed.

Ancilliary Rigging. There are two sets of tackle on Viola that are a bit special. The cutting tackle is used for hoisting in the blubber and comprises two large double-sheaved blocks. The upper block hangs at the bottom of a necklace, the ends of which pass up through the lubber holes and are lashed behind the main mast. The lower block is shackled to a large hook which is tied off out of the way when not actually in use.

The second is the cat hook tackle used for drawing up the anchor perpendicular to the catheads. Again, a fairly hefty piece of kit with double blocks (a bit smaller than those used on the cutting tackle), and a large hook. This, too, would have been lashed away when not in use.

**Fig. 10.36 Rigging to the yards.**

Fig. 10.37  Boats on davits and cranes.  The boat on bearers can be seen astern.

Fig. 10.38  The fitted out starboard whaleboat.

The hooks themselves I fashioned from 3mm thick plastic sheet. Holes were drilled for the shackle eye at the top and for the centre of the hook proper. The outline was then cut with a fret-saw and final shaping carried out with small files, remembering that hooks have a very precise shape section-wise in order to take the loads to which they are subjected. At this scale it is not really practical to get the shape mathematically correct but it must look like a proper hook and not just a bent piece of scrap material.

## Assembling the Davits and Rigging the Boats

The davits, bearers and cranes are a little vulnerable once fitted and it was essential to make sound glued and pinned joints. The cranes, which were supports hinged to the bearers, were put in the "out" position to take the boats. The boats were lashed from the bearers above, over the boat and down to ring bolts set into the hull below. Block and tackle were then added from davits to ring bolts in the top of the boats, fore and aft, see **Fig.10.37**.

I had decided to fit one of the boats out with a fairly basic set of equipment. Five pulling oars, each individually marked and of varying lengths to compensate for the curve of the boat at the gunwales, were made together with the long steering oar. Two line tubs were fitted. The smaller was left covered but the larger was exposed to show how the line, carefully coiled within the tub, ran round the loggerhead then forward to the box at the prow. The coil here was known as box warp and was, from there, connected to the first iron or harpoon. I must stress that I have used some model maker's licence in showing an exposed tub and irons in place on the crotch with the boat still on the davits. All gear would have only been deployed once the two men required to lower the boat had been joined by the rest of the crew.

## The Braces

The rigging status of the vessel calls for braces to be left a little slack and not pulled up taut. This is not a condition easy to achieve well, and one that has dogged many modellers. I have found one method that works pretty well and starts with treating the thread to be used with PVA glue and a fair amount of tension. The PVA treatment, given to all my rigging cordage is enhanced, in this case, by additional stretching. Removing most of the natural twist with my fingers first, I then hung each length up with weights and left the adhesive to dry for at least twelve hours.

Leaving the amount of desired slack in the rigging, I then tacked the line at each rigging block. The stiffened thread can then be coerced to the required catenary curve.

## The American Flag

Further research was necessary here. In 1910, the American flag had only 46 stars with the normal 13 stripes, that was not too hard to establish. What was more difficult to find out was the arrangement of the stars. Mike Doane, at Hand Made Flags, came up with 4 rows of eight, and 2 rows of seven, the latter being the second and fifth rows. This arrangement was confirmed by two other independent sources and so Hand Made Flags produced this design for me and the resultant flag was flown from the top of the main mast.

## Finishing Off

ssThere was not too much left to do at this stage and the finishing-off process comprised mainly of making and mounting coils of rope. A few points to watch here. First, make sure that the size of thread matches the falls with which the coil is associated. Secondly, remember to have enough material in the coil that would adequately work the rigging.

I touched in any paint where necessary then cleaned the decks. I had made a small flexible tube attachment to fit the household vacuum cleaner. This I use on LOW POWER. After the many hours of work put in, it would be disastrous to see some of the rigging disappear up the spout!

## Summary

As I suggested at the beginning of this project, Viola is a pretty good introduction to scratch building, particularly at 1/48 scale. There were certainly a few challenges, not the least the whaleboats. On the other hand, at this scale the rigging takes on a less fiddly aspect. The research content is a little on the high side since one has to become involved in the evolution of the American whaling industry over many years in order to better understand the working of the vessel. However, it is an interesting and fascinating subject which echoes the myths and legends as well as the very hard times at sea.

So, not only do you finish up with a rather unusual model, but you inevitably learn about a somewhat different sort of life at sea, spent under very arduous conditions.

## Acknowledgements

Many of the finer points of a technical and historical nature used in the construction of this model were established by reference to the Curator of Maritime History and used by courtesy of the Kendall Whaling Museum, Sharon, MA, U.S.A.

The inclusion of the passage from John Leavitt's book "*Charles W. Morgan*" was made with the kind permission of The Mystic Seaport Museum Inc. Mystic, CT, U.S.A.

For invaluable help with the research and production of the 1910 version of the American flag, my thanks to Mike Doane of Hand Made Flags, 64 Copse Avenue, West Wickham, Kent. BR4 9NR

## References

"*The Charles W. Morgan*" by John Leavitt, published by Mystic Seaport Publications ISBN 0-913372-10-2
"*The Whaleboat -A Study of Design, Construction and Use From 1850 - 1970*" by Willets D. Ansell, published by Mystic Seaport Publications 0-913372-40-4
The Viola - drawings by Walter E. Channing obtainable from Nancy Reardon, Museum Store, The New Bedford Whaling Museum, 18, Johnny Cake Hill, New Bedford, MA, 02740 U.S.A. Tel: 001 (508) 997 0018 The 2-sheet set (in tube) costs $18 inc. shipping. IMO, Visa or Mastercard acceptable.

# CHAPTER 11

# ANOTHER LOOK AT RIGGING

I think that first of all, it should be said that the rigging of a static model does not have to be the fearful task it is believed to be by so many potential model makers. I agree that the fully rigged model does look somewhat awesome in its content, but that appearance has often more to do with amount than with complexity. When it is realised that every piece of rigging does a specific job, then much of the apparent maze tends to take on a more sensible perspective.

There are two distinct types of rigging: those ropes that hold masts, bowsprit, etc., in permanent position, known collectively as the standing rigging, and those that move spars and sails about, known collectively as the running rigging. The former normally uses black thread to simulate the ropes tarred for protection against the elements, and the latter, tan-coloured thread to represent the natural hemp ropes that had to be reeved through blocks and other tackle. Most kits worth their salt will provide threads of the appropriate size and colour. If not, then you have to resort to dyeing as required.

Having raised the subject of thread, let us consider some of the properties we should either avoid or overcome. First of all, try not to use nylons or polyesters: they are very much dust magnets, sometimes do not have the ability to hold a knot or lashing and frequently have a resistance to adhesives. Cotton can be another no-no, because of its tendency to stretch. These are seldom found in kits and the problem usually arises if you should run out and have to seek a source of supply from your local haberdashers where linen thread is the best option. At the end of the day you are probably best advised to get supplies from a reputable model boat shop.

You will need several different thicknesses of cordage dependent upon the scale of your model. In general, standing rigging is thicker at the lower mast level and gets increasingly thinner as you rise up to the mast head. Pretty much the same applies to running rigging, but there are exceptions, so scan your drawings and parts lists well.

Having got your thread, try to resist taking lengths straight off the coil to do your rigging. Even under a low-powered magnifying glass, you will see thousands of very tiny hairs sticking up from the surface of the thread. Each one of these invites a bit of dust to hang on it. I have found that the easiest way to get rid of these is to give the thread what I call the PVA treatment. I put a blob of PVA adhesive between the pads of thumb and forefinger, them pull the thread through. This per-

forms two very distinct functions. This fixes all the little hairs down to the surface of the thread and, just as importantly, depending upon how tight you grip with thumb and forefinger, you will take out much of the natural twist which can be a very definite aid to rigging. As you put tension on a block and tackle, for instance, the natural twist is drawn out and torque is built up in the system. Then, when you tie off, some of the tension is released and everything tends to spring back into a horrible twisted mess. An extension to the PVA treatment is to apply and maintain tension to the thread with weights while the adhesive dries. This is particularly advantageous for those parts of the rigging where the lines are required to be left slack. Without some sort of treatment, thread straight off the reel will not take up that nice looking catenary curve that is formed by the weight of the rope hanging between two points at different levels.

Before leaving the subject of rigging thread, it should be noted that there was shroud-laid rope, (right hand twist) and cable-laid rope, (left hand twist). If you want to build your model to incorporate that degree of detail and recognise that difference where pertinent, you will almost certainly have to lay your own rope. I do not know of any proprietary source which offers model makers threads specifically laid left hand.

Another area of rigging that causes some concern to model makers is the application of foot ropes and stirrups, the latter usually being the source of trouble. The difficulty arises from the fact that thread over such a short length has a mind of it's own and invariably refuses to hang straight down without kinking. One of the better solutions is to make a technical adjustment to the material selection (cheat) and use soft florists' wire. This provides a stability that not only enables the right hang of the stirrup, but it also keeps them all in line across the spar and assists in attaining an even sag throughout the length of the foot rope.

I mentioned above that the hairs standing up on untreated thread could be seen under a low-power glass. There are several places in the rigging process where such a glass can enhance the operation, setting up lanyards between deadeyes on smaller scale projects for instance. Hobbies (Dereham) Limited, Dereham, Norfolk NR19 2QZ, can supply a magnifying lamp with a daylight simulation bulb which I have personally found to be most useful.

I would refer the reader to the previous two Handbooks in

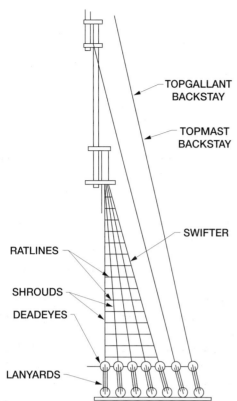

**Fig. 11.1**

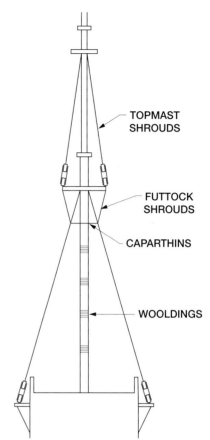

**Fig. 11.2**

this series of publications for details of "hands on" methods of actually putting up the rigging. However, one aspect of the subject does deserve further comment - whether or not to have sails on the model. The decision can be influenced by two factors. If the aim of your model is to demonstrate the correct and proper sailing mechanisms of the real thing then, I guess, sails are a must. If, however, you are not constrained by that degree of completeness, then the choice is far more open.

If you are looking for visual realism then, strictly speaking, the only model that should have a full set of sails, is the waterline model set in a diorama or artificial sea. However, realism in that sense is not always a factor for the modeller and there are many justifiable areas of licence. You have only to look at some of the fine models in the National Maritime Museum that do not even have masts! Discussions about the rights and wrongs of the matter have been going on for so long now, without definitive resolution, that you are left to set your own target as to what your model is to achieve. If that aim is fulfilled then, in my opinion, you should be happy to repel all boarders! What is important, is that you must recognise that the rigging content will increase with the presence of sails. Leave them off and some of the associated running rigging can also be disregarded. Remember too, that the position of yards on the masts will also differ for the two conditions.

So, what rigging can be left off if you decide not to fit sails? This is a little bit of a difficult question to answer. Much will depend on the type and size of vessel in question and to the reasons for unbending the sails in the first place. Putting gear back up is quite a time-consuming task and so it is probable that the amount of running rigging taken down is largely relative to the amount of time the vessel will be in dock. As for the model, the standing rigging will not be affected and neither will the running rigging that relates to the control of yards and spars. As a general rule of thumb, it will only be

those parts of the running rigging that pertain to the sails that should be considered for omission. Buntlines, bowlines and brails immediately come to mind. Sheets and tacks for any fore and aft sails are also likely candidates, those for courses and square sails were hauled up out of the way by the clue lines and clue garnets and would not, therefore, be left off but clue'd up. The next question that arises is whether or not to omit the blocks that would be used for the rigging that you have decided to leave off. If your model is competition bound, my advice would be to play safe and leave them on. At least you have told the judge that you have thought about it.

It will always help to have some idea as to what the various lines do in the overall rigging picture. The following terms and descriptions are given to assist in that better understanding. The line drawings are not to scale, nor do they represent any particular type of vessel, but are hopefully sufficient to illustrate the position and use of the items concerned.

## Rigging Terminology

**Backstays. Fig.11.1** Ropes that descend from all mastheads to the sides of the vessel below. They are usually set up with deadeyes and lanyards to the aft end of the channels or chain wales. They take the strain on the upper masts.

**Bobstays. Fig.11.2** These may be either of rope or chain and run from the underside of the bowsprit down to the stem of the hull. The bobstay restrains the bowsprit in a downward direction to counteract the upper pull of the foremast stays.

**Boom Topping Lift. Fig.11.3** A rope that lifts a boom at its outer end. It runs from the outer end of the boom to a block at the masthead above then down, via further tackle to the adjacent channels or bulwarks.

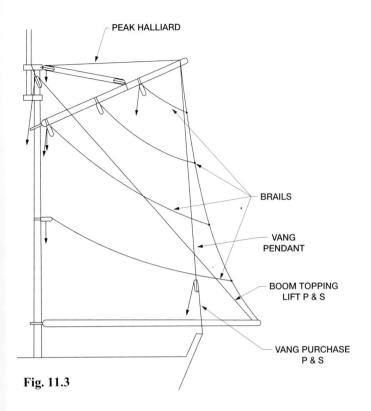

**Fig. 11.3**

**Bowlines and Bridles. Fig.11.4** The bridle is a rope device secured to the side edges of a square sail and to which the bowline is attached. The bowline runs forward to keep the weather edge of the sail under control when the vessel is close hauled.

**Braces & Brace Pendants. Fig.11.4** The pendant is a length of rope fixed to the outer ends of the yard arms, its other end stropped onto a block. The brace itself is rove through the block and used to traverse the yards horizontally.

**Brails. Fig.11.3** Ropes attached to the foot or back edge of a mizen, try-sail or stay-sail, running through blocks on the gaff above, then on down to deck. Used to haul in sail to mast and gaff. Similar to the furling of a square sail.

**Buntlines. Fig.11.4** Lines attached to the foot of square sails that then run up over the forward face of the sail to blocks on the yard above, along to the masthead, then down to deck level. Used to control the foot of the sail and haul up the sail when furling.

**Caparthins. Fig.11.2** Ropes that hold the upper port and starboard shrouds from spreading apart. Usually applied at the lower end of the futtock shrouds.

**Clue Garnets. Fig.11.4** These ropes are used to haul up the lower corners, or clues, of the courses when furling. These are the square sails that hang below the main and fore yards.

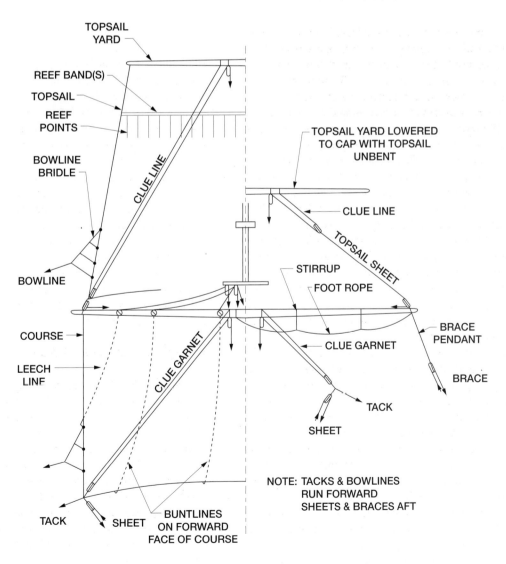

**Fig. 11.4**

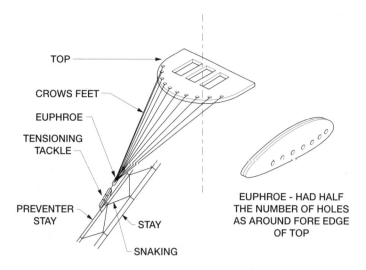

**Fig. 11.5**

**Clue Lines. Fig.11.4** Similar to clue garnets but applied to the upper square sails.

**Collar. Fig.11.6** A length of rope around the bowsprit into which is seized a deadeye or heart. A stay with a similar fitting at its lower end is drawn up tight with a lanyard.

**Crows Foot. Fig.11.5** A series of ropes rove through a euphroe block rigged to a stay that splay out to the front edge of a top. They prevent chafing of the bottom edge of the sail above.

**Downhaul. Fig.11.6** As inferred by its name, a rope fixed to the head of a fore-and-aft sail and used for hauling it down when furling.

**Euphroe Block. Fig.11.5** A long multiholed block through which is rove the crows foot.

**Fife Rail.** A rail for belaying pins set up on pillars or stanchions around the bottom of a mast. Similar to a pin rail which fixes to the inside of the bulwarks.

**Foot Rope. Fig.11.4** A rope suspended by stirrups below a yard on which sailors can stand when working the sails.

**Fore-and-Aft Sails.** Those rigged along the centre line of the vessel.

**Futtock Shrouds. Fig.11.2** Stays in the form of chain, rope or iron rods that run from the mast to the outside of a top or crosstrees and attached to the lower deadeyes of the upper shrouds. In some instances the lower ends are attached to the lower shrouds rather than the mast. The style of fitting is largely dependent on the period of the vessel concerned.

**Gammoning.** A length of rope attached to the bowsprit then passed through a hole in the stem of the vessel and back up over the bowsprit. Up to ten turns are made keeping the turns to forward on the bowsprit and aft through the hole in the stem. The same number of frapping turns is made around the middle of the gammoning to draw the system up taut.

**Halliard. Fig.11.6** A rope for hoisting sails. (The opposite function to a downhaul). Term can also be applied to yards and flags.

**Head Stays. Fig.11.6** Those stays that are rigged between the bowsprit and the foremast.

**Horse.** A bar that runs transversely across the deck on which slides a block to which is attached the sheet of a fore-and-aft sail.

**Jeers.** A heavy duty block and tackle system used to support the centre of a yard. Also used for lowering the yard if required. Sometimes used in conjunction with a sling.

**Lanyard. Fig.11.1 & 11.6** A rope rove between the deadeyes for tightening up shrouds and stays.

**Leech Lines Fig.11.4** Ropes attached to the side or leech of a

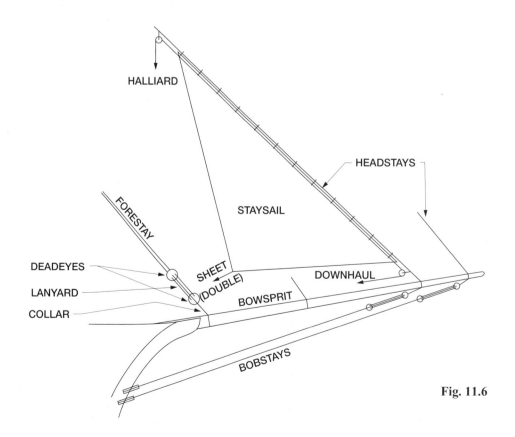

**Fig. 11.6**

square sail and used to truss the sails very close up to the yard.

**Lifts**. These take the weight of a yard when it is down on the caps and sails are furled. Used for hoisting the yard back into sailing position.

**Parrals**. A series of two or three rows of ribs and trucks attached to a yard either side of the mast and around it in order to enhance transverse movement of the yard.

**Peak Halliards. Fig.11.3** Similar to a boom topping lift but applied to the gaff above.

**Pin Rail**. A rail fixed to the inside of the bulwarks with holes for belaying pins. See also fife rail.

**Preventer Stay. Fig.11.5** An auxiliary stay usually rigged below the basic stay and often snaked to it. Comes into its own if the stay is shot away in battle.

**Puddening**. Usually in the form of a rope served around the anchor ring to prevent chafing. In more general terms, can be scrap material applied to rails or stays against which the edges of sails might rub.

**Ratlines. Fig.11.1** Ropes across the shrouds that provide the means for sailors to get aloft. (The model makers nightmare).

**Reef Bands. Fig.11.4** Narrow reinforcing bands of canvas across a sail supporting eyelets through which the reef points pass.

**Reef Points. Fig.11.4** Short lengths of line attached to the fore and aft faces of a sail. They are used for tying a reefed sail to the yard.

**Sheet. Fig.11.4** A rope that runs aft from the lower corners of a sail down to deck used in the control of the sail.

**Shrouds. Fig.11.1** Rigging between the lower mast head and the bulwarks or channels. There is a precise order in which these are set up, the fore starboard pair followed by the fore port pair, then back to starboard etc. They are tightened up by lanyards between deadeyes at their lower end. Upper shrouds are similarly rigged at top-mast and top-gallant levels via futtock shrouds.

**Snaking. Fig.11.5** A feature of 18th century rigging which linked stays and their preventers together by means of a rope seized zig-zag fashion to both.

**Sling**. A rope or chain that takes the weight of a yard that doesn't move up or down on its mast.

**Stays. Fig.11.5** Ropes rigged fore and aft to support the masts. See also backstays.

**Stirrups. Fig.11.4** Short ropes or straps that hang from the rear side of a yard to support the foot ropes.

**Swifter. Fig.11.1** The aft-most shroud when the number of shrouds is uneven. It is attached to the masthead using an eye splice.

**Tack. Fig.11.4** A rope that runs forward from, and to control, the lower corners of a course.

**Truss**. A rope system for tying a yard to a mast while letting it move transversely. A simple version of parrals but without ribs and trucks. The ends of the rope are taken either down to deck or up to the back end of trestle trees above.

**Vangs. Fig.11.3** Ropes running from the end of a gaff, via tackle, to either side of the deck below. Used to control the gaff from side to side.

**Woolding. Fig.11.2** Rope reinforcement wound around a mast. About 12in wide, these bands of rope are usually contained, top and bottom by narrow wooden washers. These were superseded by iron bands around 3in wide at the end of the 18th century.

The above list is by no means complete but should help the model maker identify the most common ropes that are likely to be encountered. I have tried to define the features using as much plain English as possible.

## Rigging Do's and Don'ts

Some of the ongoing points may seem fairly obvious and some of them even appear in earlier chapters of this book. However, I make no apologies for repeating them because I know at my cost that we all tend to take short cuts or, indeed, think we are cleverer than we really are!

**DO** remove your wrist-watch and rings before starting to rig. There are all sorts of little protrusions that can get caught up without you realising. It's only when you move your hand away from the model.........!

**DO** roll your sleeves up or wear a short sleeve shirt. Cuffs and their buttons can cause almost as much havoc as a watch.

**DO** make sure that your scalpel blades, or whatever cutting tools you use, are sharp. Blunt tools mean more effort and less control when you are amongst all the rigging.

**DO** treat and tension your rigging thread before tying it on.

**DO** make sure that the holes through all blocks are clear before lashing them in position. A partially obstructed hole will always be in a block that is in a more inaccessible place. That bloke Murphy has much to answer for! A smear of cyanoacrylate on the end of the rope being rove will stiffen it to form a sort of built-in bodkin - worth doing anyway whether or not you have got a blocked hole.

**DO** try to ensure that all blocks are of the same material. Proprietary blocks are usually in boxwood or walnut. Mixing them up just doesn't look right on a model ship.

**DO** use a paper template to establish spacing of ratlines. The eye can be misled by the converging verticals of the shrouds which can lead to progressively uneven spacing. Placing such a template between mast and shrouds also helps to eliminate strain on the eyes.

**DO** put up the ratlines in easy stages. DON'T leave them all until the end.

**DO** rewind any hanked threads supplied in kits onto reels or cards. This avoids tangles at a later date. Tangles and knots will always be at a point about 2in short of the length you want. (That guy Murphy again).

**DO** try to work in good light. Black thread is not the easiest to focus on if you are working in poor illumination.

**DON'T** open the blades of scissors or other cutters until the cutting area has reached the thread you want to trim. If you can pull the end to be trimmed taut with a pair of tweezers in the other hand, so much the better. At least that way you are fairly sure by feel that you are cutting the right thread!

**DON'T** soak knots in cyanoacrylate by applying the nozzle to the knot. After all, you are only trying to stop it from coming undone and all that is needed is the merest touch with a toothpick or similar applicator. There are rumours that soaked knots degrade after a period of time and the adjacent threads become brittle and snap. This could be scuttlebut of course. I have used cyanoacrylate since it became commercially available and have, as yet, not suffered adversely. But then, I always use a toothpick.

I mentioned earlier that there are some ropes that look better if left slack. Braces, sheets and tacks are prominent in this category. To get anything like a natural-looking curve you must stiffen the thread being used and a thorough soaking in slightly diluted PVA is ideal. The thread is then hung up with weights for about twenty-four hours to let the adhesive go right off. The condition is then such as to permit the gentle coercion of curves into the thread, not forgetting of course, that while you are teasing the curve in one plane, in the other plane the thread has to remain flat. This is not too much of a problem where you are dealing with a single rope slung between two points, but where the rope has to be rove through blocks, a different technique can sometimes be in order. In such cases, where the passage of the thread through the block can tend to straighten the curve so patiently acquired, I reckon that it is acceptable to use model makers licence, or in true terms, cheat. On these occasions, the thread from the first point of suspension to the entry of the hole in the block is made from a separate piece. The thread that comes out of the block is a different piece altogether. That means that you can present two slightly different curves into the system and add to the realism. The curve, or catenary, that is subtended by a rope hanging freely between two points at different levels will vary in a system of rigging.

A further feature of rigging a model boat is the flying of a flag. All too often, a well-built model is spoilt by lack of attention to this important facet. Quite frankly, I would prefer to see a model without a flag rather than see a flag that has been put on almost as an afterthought. The first requirement is to get the right flag for the type of vessel and the period concerned. A typical example of the research required is demonstrated in the model of Viola in Chapter 10. Not only was it necessary to determine the number of stars on the 1910 version of the American flag, but to also find out their arrangement. Who is going to look or count? If you enter a model competitively into some exhibitions, I know at least two judges who will.

Having got your flag to the correct design, then it needs to be shaped to look as if it has a breeze of some sort blowing through it. You don't want it to look like the American Stars and Stripes that was planted during the first lunar landing! There are all sorts of dodges that can be used. Soaking to soften the material, manipulation between thumb and forefinger to generate the gentle folds followed by spraying with hair lacquer is one method. There are several, but the choice can depend upon the nature of the flag material or just plain personal preference.

Finally, do fly the flag in the correct place. There are certain places for certain flags, particularly when dealing with naval vessels.

## References

"*The Masting and Rigging of English Ships of War*" by James Lees, published by Conway Maritime Press ISBN 0 85177 290 0

"*Eighteenth-century Rigs and Rigging*" by Karl Heinz Marquardt, published by Conway Maritime Press ISBN 0 85177 586 1

"*Sailing Ship Rigs and Rigging*" by Harold A. Underhill, published by Brown, Son & Ferguson Ltd. ISBN 0 85174 176 2

"*Flags at Sea*" by Timothy Wilson, published by Chatham Publishing ISBN 1 86176 116 3

# INDEX

Adhesives    10, 20, 26, 34, 42 45, 56, 70, 90, 113, 142, 157
Anchors    31, 74

Backstays    182
Balustrading    99
Bellona    10
Blocks    30, 31
Boat cranes    169
Boats    149, 171
Bobstays    182
Boom topping lift    182
Bowline    183
Bowsprit    50, 135, 149, 169
Bowsprit rigging    31
Bounty    141
Bounty - Jolly Boat    111
Braces    183
Brails    183
Bulkheads (Frames)    34, 56, 90, 131, 143, 161, 174
Buntlines    183
Burton pendants    31
Bulwarks    22
Bulwark rails    26, 39, 57, 70, 93, 94, 161, 165

Caparthins    183
Caulking    20
Chainplates    28, 60, 70, 101
Channels    28, 42, 60
Chimney    42, 147
Clue Garnets    183
Clue lines    185
Collar    185
Crosstrees    30, 124, 171
Crowsfeet    31, 185

Davits    169
Deadeyes    30
Deck fittings    24
Deck Planking    20, 22, 35, 58, 92, 134, 143, 161
Decoration    26, 41, 97
Downhaul    184

Elbe    67

Euphroe blocks    31, 184

False keel    34, 56, 69, 90, 113, 131, 143, 174
Fife rail    184
Figurehead    42, 50
Flags    31, 52, 63, 179
Foot rope    184
Fore and aft sails    184
Frame assembly    13, 34, 35, 69
Frame edge shaping    14, 35
Frames (Bulkheads)    34, 56, 90, 113, 131, 143, 161, 174
Futtock shrouds    30, 152, 184

Gammoning    50, 51, 184
Gratings    24, 42, 58, 100
Gun carriage    28, 39, 100, 145, 147
Gun-ports    20, 42, 94, 96, 123, 145
Gun-port lids    96

Halliard    184
Headrails    26, 42, 45, 46, 60, 97, 98, 148
Head stays    184
Head timbers    24, 45
Horse    184

Jackstays    169, 171
Jeers    184
Jolly Boat    111

Knightheads    26

Lanyards    184
Leech lines    184
Lifts    185

Marking out    159
Mast caps    30
Masts    28, 30, 50, 61, 102, 115, 124, 136, 149, 171
Material selection    156

Netting    175

Oars    172

Ornamentation                                     26, 41, 97

Parrels                                                        185
Peak halliards                                                 185
Pendants, Burton                                                31
Pin rail                                                       185
Plank bending                  17, 19, 57, 69, 90, 133, 145, 163
Planking            14, 17, 19, 35, 36, 39, 57, 69, 91, 114, 121,
                                         133, 145, 163, 174
Plasticard                                                167, 169
Poop deck rails                                                 28
Portsmouth                                                      55
Preventer stay                                                 185
Pride of Baltimore                                             129
Puddening                                                      185

Ratlines                               31, 51, 52, 152, 175, 185
Reef bands                                                     185
Reef points                                                    185
Research                                                       156
Rigging                                                        181
Rigging terminology                                            182
Roundhouses                                                     26
Running rigging                31, 52, 77, 117, 137, 152, 175

Sails                                                74, 77, 116
San Felipe                                                      85
Sheathing                                      15, 16, 145, 163
Sheet                                                          185
Shrouds                                        30, 51, 152, 185
Snaking                                                        185
Sling                                                          185

Spars (Yards)   30, 50, 61, 115, 124, 126, 127, 149, 171, 177
Spiral staircase                                               99
Standing rigging                    30, 31, 51, 61, 77, 117, 126,
                                         136, 151, 152, 174
Stays                                                          185
Stirrups                                                       185
Swifter                                                        185

Tack                                                           185
Timber-heads                                                    26
Tools              10, 34, 56, 69, 89, 112, 121, 131, 142
Tops                                                     151, 171
Trestletrees                                                    30
Truss                                                          185
Try works                                                      167

Unicorn

Vangs                                                          185
Varnish                                                         41
Victory section                                                119
Viola                                                          155

Whaleboats
         Construction                                          171
         Equipment                                             172
         Fitting out                                           174
Windlass                                                       167
Woldings (Woolding)                                       30, 185

Yards (Spars)   30, 50, 61, 115, 124, 126, 127, 149, 171, 177